*The real picture of how it had been there*
*and how we had been there*
*was in our minds, bright with sun and*
*wet with sea water and blue or burned,*
*and the whole crusted over*
*with exploring thought.*

*John Steinbeck, The Log from The* Sea of Cortez

# Loreto
## Baja California Sur, Mexico

Alan Axelrod, David Axelrod, and Aaron Bodansky

Best Guides LLC

*Best Guide: Loreto*

Alan Axelrod, David Axelrod, and Aaron Bodansky

Printed and bound in Canada by Hemlock Printers, Inc.
First edition published in 2007.

*Designer:* Paulette Eickman, Seattle, Washington
*Editor:* Leslie Eliel, Seattle, Washington
*Photographer:* Doug Ogle, Seattle, Washington
Additional Photographer Credits on pages 191 & 192

ISBN: 978-0-9700455-8-4

For information or to order additional copies of this book, please contact:
Best Guides LLC, 2100 North Pacific Street, Seattle, WA 98103
Phone 206-428-4350
www.bestguideloreto.com

FRONT COVER PHOTOS—*Top:* Pangas in early morning. *Bottom:* Paletas (popsickles) at La Michoacana. See page 57 for review. Photos by Doug Ogle

BACK COVER PHOTOS—*Top:* Desert vista south of Loreto. *Bottom:* Sunrise in Loreto harbor. *Logo Inset:* Mission bell tower. Photos by Doug Ogle

INSIDE FRONT COVER PHOTO—Cloud over Isla Santa Catalina, Bay of Loreto National Marine Park, Sea of Cortés, Baja California. ©Jack Swenson, www.BajaPhotos.com

# LORETO: "WHERE THE MOUNTAINS COME TO SWIM"

The first time I visited Loreto, I found a town with remarkable natural beauty, rustic charm, a rich history, and friendly people. The available Baja California travel guides included only a few pages on Loreto. I was inspired to offer more. I enlisted the help of my friend Aaron Bodansky and together we explored the town and the surrounding area. We ate at every restaurant, interviewed every outfitter, hit every pothole, met many people in the expat community, and befriended many native Loretanos. We started our research as foreigners, but when finished we felt like a part of the community. What is included in the following pages is all that we

Authors Aaron Bodansky, left and David Axelrod, right.

discovered—all the practical information you need and all the basics, as well as many secrets and hidden gems we felt were important to share. This book is for everyone who comes to Loreto, from first-time visitors to homeowners.

Loreto is a fascinating small town that is going through a profound transformation of growth and celebrity. It is a quiet, funky fishing village and an historic Spanish mission town rich in religious and historical importance. Bordered on one side by the Sierra de la Giganta (*sierra* means "mountain range") and on the other by the emerald waters of the Sea of Cortés, native legend refers to Loreto as "the place where the mountains come to swim." It is a growing tourist destination, luring travelers with its many offerings—sport fishing, kayaking, whale watching, diving, hiking, biking, off-roading, sun-worshipping, and general adventuring for all ages. It is also a real-estate destination. Seven miles (11 km) south of town a sustainable development in progress called the

Villages of Loreto Bay offers those who fall in love with the area a place to put down roots.

There is so much to explore in Loreto: the perfect mix of a tranquil beach town and an ecological adventure mecca, with traditional Mexican culture and exquisite natural beauty to boot. Enjoy your time here. Be prepared for a very laid back pace of life. Don't be surprised if a store or taco stand closes early because the owner decided to go on vacation. Be patient, you're in Loreto. We love Loreto, and we're confident you will too—especially with *Best Guide: Loreto* in hand.

*David Axelrod*

 **How to Use This Book**

Information about Loreto is changing rapidly. Restaurants and bars open and close regularly or just change names. New establishments and businesses of all types are popping up every month. Although the URLs, e-mail information, location and hours of operation presented were current as of the date of publication, the only guarantee we can provide is that the information contained herein is constantly changing.

To accommodate this fluid situation we have created a new interactive website to accompany this guidebook and keep the information fresh. Users of this book who would like to contribute information or opinions about their experiences in Loreto or who want to sign up for automatic updates are encouraged to go to *www.bestguideloreto.com* to be a part of the *Best Guide: Loreto* user community.

The authors have done their best to include as many businesses as possible in the various categories of goods and services reviewed. They are listed under each section in alphabetical order. If there are any new or old businesses that we missed but who would like to be considered for the next printing, please send us your contact information.

All money references in *Best Guide: Loreto* marked by $ refer to U.S. dollars, even though Canadian dollars and Mexican pesos also use this symbol. (So if you see an order of huevos rancheros going for $50 you might want to remember to move the decimal point one digit to the left for a general idea of the price.) In the book, reference to prices in pesos will use the format "100 pesos." American currency is accepted just about everywhere currently on a 10:1 exchange rate. This, of course, allows a 10% advantage to the Mexican vendor given that the exchange rate (at the time of printing) is closer to 11:1.

# TABLE OF CONTENTS

# TABLE OF CONTENTS

Long-Beaked Common Dolphins    **3**

4    A Grey Whale calf rolling on its mother, a common behavior of calves.

Short-Finned Pilot Whale

Humpback Whale Breach

Sea Lion

Sally Lightfoot Crabs

Striped Marlin

Green Sea Turtle

Gulf Stars

A favorite island kayak camp in the protected bay of Loreto National Marine Park.

Loreto, named after the Latin for laurel grove, has many narrow streets shaded by sculptured laurel trees.

# 1

# An Introduction to Loreto

- Loreto's Story: A Quick History
- Changes Impacting Loreto Today

# LORETO'S STORY: A QUICK HISTORY

## The Indigenous People

When Christian missionaries first arrived in Loreto, there were three distinct groups of native people on the peninsula: the **Pericú**, who lived from the tip of the Baja California peninsula to the area around modern day La Paz; the **Guaycura**, who lived northward from there to the Loreto area; and the **Cochimí**, who lived from Loreto all the way up the remainder of the peninsula. Thus, the Jesuit priests landed in an area on the boundaries of two indigenous Indian nations. The missions appealed to the native people who relied on them for food, and their conversion was relatively easy. The total native population of Loreto at this time was around 400.

The settlement of Loreto marked the beginning of the end for the indigenous people of the peninsula. It is estimated there were about 4,000 inhabitants in the area at the beginning of the eighteenth century. The population of the entire peninsula was approximately 45,000. European diseases quickly ravaged the local peoples in a series of epidemics in the 1700s. It is ironic that the very people who supposedly needed "saving" were instead annihilated over the course of time. By the end of the nineteenth century there were only a few mixed European-Guaycura in Loreto. By the end of the twentieth century the Guaycura and Pericú were extinct. Fortunately, some of their language has survived; today, most place names bear both the Spanish and the Indian names together. For example, the full name of the mission at San Javier is called San Francisco Javier de Viggé Biaundó: the mountains west of Loreto were known to the Cochimí as Viggé, and the San Javier area was known as Biaundó.

## The First Europeans

**Hernando Cortés** first explored Baja California in 1533. Lack of food and water drove the Spaniards away and kept them away for the next 150 years. The next attempt to establish a European settlement in the Loreto area was made by **Jesuit Padre Eusebio Kino** in 1684 at San Bruno, 12 miles (19 km) north of Loreto, but the effort also ended in failure due to the inadequate water supply. On October 18, 1697, **Padre Juan María Salvatierra** returned and landed in Loreto with a garrison of about seventeen soldiers under his command.

## Name That Family

The impact of European colonialism and American emigration to Loreto is most apparent in the local family names. Surprisingly, much of the population has English surnames including Davis, Cunningham, Green, Smith, and Drew.

*Davis.* The biggest family in Loreto is the Davis family. The first Davises who arrived in Loreto in 1820 were two brothers, Pedro and Lucas. Although Lucas fathered several girls, Pedro had three sons who in turn had large families of mostly boys. Today, about 40% of the population is related, with Davis as one of their two last names (two last names are standard in Spanish lineage). There are even some residents with the surnames "Davis Davis" in Loreto.

If you meet someone in the Davis family in Loreto, make sure to pronounce it "dah-VEES" rather than the typical American pronunciation "DAY-vis." This is important to them because they want to emphasize their Mexican heritage. On Davis Street, one block inland from the Malecón, many members of the namesake family have homes. However, because the families tended to build in the backyards of the preceding Davis generation, there are dozens of homes hidden in the huge compounds behind the street-front homes.

*Cunningham.* William Stuart Cunningham came from New York as an 18-year-old in 1857 to help his mother. She had remarried an English engineer who later abandoned her in Loreto when their copper mine stopped producing. William worked the mine with his mother for a few more years and then turned to ranching. He bought nearly 20,000 hectares of land (in what was then the middle of nowhere), and, with his wife and four children, raised livestock and sold wood for the copper furnaces in Santa Rosalía.

After his wife passed away, Cunningham remarried and had twelve more children. Four generations later, people still ask today's Cunninghams which side of the family they are from, the original family or the second one.

Across from the mission on the cobblestone shopping zone of Avenida Salvatierra, is a building previously owned by William Cunningham so that his children could go to school in town. It is built on the foundations of one of the earliest structures in Loreto built by Padre Jaime Bravo, an assistant to Padre Salvatierra, around 1720.

By the end of the seventeenth century, the nearly bankrupt Spanish throne had good reasons for exploring and colonizing Baja California. First, thinking at one time that the peninsula was an island, the Spanish sought a northern shortcut trade route to the Far East. It was also looking for a good port of call for its Pacific Ocean-crossing galleons. Lastly, it wanted a buffer against the encroaching Russians from the north and from the English who roamed the world's oceans.

## La Misión Nuestra Señora de Loreto

**Padre Kino** encouraged his friend and fellow priest **Juan María Salvatierra** to found a mission called Our Lady of Loreto in the California wilderness. Although he attempted to return to Padre Kino's original site in San Bruno, Padre Salvatierra ultimately founded the mission, **La Misión Nuestra Señora de Loreto**, in 1697, making it the first permanent Spanish settlement in the Californias.

The Jesuits founded eighteen missions on the Baja California peninsula during their seventy-year presence in the Californias. As the Loreto colony grew, it served as a base for California exploration and for the expansion of the mission system throughout the peninsula. **Franciscan Padre Junípero Serra** started his journey north to California from here in 1769, eventually founding Alta California's first mission at San Diego Bay and the now-famous chain of missions throughout mainland California and the American Southwest. The missionary work of the Franciscans only lasted for six years, however, before the King of Spain had them replaced by the Dominican order in 1773.

## The Town of Loreto

Loreto continued to serve as the Californias' secular and religious capital for 132 years. Superseded by La Paz following an 1829 hurricane, Loreto remained virtually deserted until the 1850s and 1860s when a small group of immigrants, including some from England, resettled the area. A surprising number of Loreto residents today bear surnames from these pioneers, names such as Green, Davis, Cunningham, and Drew. Loreto remained a frontier backwater until after World War II, when it began developing a small commercial and sportfishing industry.

The 1973 the **Transpeninsular Highway** finally made the area accessible to the average tourist. Today Loreto is part of a seventeen-mile (27-km) coastal segment, including **Nopoló** and **Puerto Escondido**,

## La Misión Nuestra Señora de Loreto

"This Lady, of plaster and wood and paint, is one of the strong ecological factors of the town of Loreto, and not to know her and her strength is to fail to know Loreto. She may disappear and her name be lost, as the Magna Mater, as Isis, have disappeared. But something very like her will take her place, and the longings which created her will find somewhere in the world a similar altar on which to pour their force. She is as eternal as our species, and we will continue to manufacture her as long as we survive."

John Steinbeck, *The Log from The Sea of Cortez*

These statues stand behind the main altar at La Misión Nuestra Señora de Loreto.

Loreto Malecón

long slated by the Mexican government for development as a major tourist resort area. In the town itself, a restored cobblestone plaza adjoins the historic mission church and museum (the town's tallest building), and a *malecón* (boardwalk) has transformed the old seawall into a picturesque promenade.

Loreto is much more than it appears at first glance. Most visitors never make it out of the historic center of town. But things are changing and development is under way both north and south of town. The municipality already has completed a major regional plan. To the north, beyond the end of the paved road, many homes have been built on or near the beach. Just north of this enclave, a new inland marina has been approved and a beautiful stretch of beach seems destined for homes, hotels, and tourism. To the south, the **Zaragoza** neighborhood across the Río Loreto (a huge arroyo) is also a modestly visited poorer section of town. Improvements are in the works, including a new paved street and the addition of sewers, and several properties have been slated for redevelopment.

# CHANGES IMPACTING LORETO TODAY

## Fonatur's Vision

**Fonatur** (Fondo Nacional de Fomento al Turismo), Mexico's national trust for the promotion of tourism, celebrated its thirtieth anniversary in 2004. In that short time, it has managed to mastermind the infrastructure behind modern tourism in Mexico by developing some prime coastal real estate and encouraging foreign investment in its projects. During its history, Fonatur has developed five of Mexico's top beach resort areas—**Cancún**, **Ixtapa**, **Los Cabos**, **Huatulco**, and now **Loreto**—ushering in a new era for Mexican tourism.

In many respects, Loreto still remains the wonderfully funky and laid-back fishing village it has been for decades. The challenge in the ensuing years will be to retain this old world charm as the area goes through major growth and expansion.

## Development at Nopoló

Seven miles (11 km) south of Loreto, the region of **Nopoló** sits in the corridor of Loreto between the magnificent **Sierra de la Giganta** and the peaceful **Sea of Cortés**. Fonatur saw in Nopoló's sandy beaches and transparent blue water the potential for a world-class tourism destination, and marked it for development.

In the early eighties, Fonatur invested in a golf course and championship tennis facility, modernized Loreto's infrastructure, built an international airport, and constructed full marina facilities at Puerto Escondido, 16 miles (26 km) south of town. For various reasons the project sat idle until the **Loreto Bay Company**—a joint Mexican, American, and Canadian venture—with the assistance of Fonatur, came along to create a sustainable mega-development in the Nopoló area. The development

called The **Villages of Loreto Bay** has been a major part of the renewed interest in the area and is bringing homes, condos, and other facilities to the region, along with a vacation rental program. With it is coming an influx of new airplane routes to the area.

Newly constructed homes in The Villages of Loreto Bay.

The Villages of Loreto Bay (*www.loretobay.com*) is a mixed-use, health-oriented, resort-lifestyle town along 3 miles (5 km) of Nopoló beachfront. It is today the largest sustainable development under construction in North America. Loreto Bay Company intends to design, develop, and market the project on over 3,000 acres of land with more than 5,000 additional acres of land remaining dedicated as a "green lands" preserve. When completed, in nine phases over the next ten to fifteen years, the town is expected to consist of approximately 6,000 homes in a range of types and sizes in several carefully planned, pedestrian-oriented villages, each with a distinct identity and character. A commercial/retail component of the project is under construction in the "Founder's Neighborhood" to provide for the lifestyle needs of the community and the area.

Loreto Bay's commitment to the principles of environmental sustainability, architectural beauty, and human-scale planning, and to opportunities for lifelong vitality and growth, seeks to distinguish the development. Clearly, property owners are primarily American, Canadian, and Mexican baby boomers looking to be a part of an environmentally, socially, and economically sustainable resort community.

## Loreto Bay National Marine Park

The marine park encompasses Loreto's five nearby islands—**Coronado**, **Carmen**, **Danzante**, **Santa Catalina**, and **Monserrat**—and the surrounding waters of the bay. Formalizing a much-needed consensus on how the area's natural resources are to be used, **Loreto Bay National Marine Park** (Parque Nacional Marino Bahía de Loreto) was established in order to find a balance between commercial and recreational (sport) interests, such as fishing, diving, and boating. It took sixty meetings, conducted over the course of two years, for interested parties to agree on the rules and regulations before **President Ernesto Zedillo** officially authorized the park's creation in 1996. Every detail was debated and ruled on, from fishing nets' depth, size, and distance away from shore to the boundaries of jet-ski-restricted zones.

The primary purpose of the marine park is to promote and stimulate conservation awareness. Because the marine life in Loreto Bay is some of the most diverse in the world, the park seeks to protect the natural habitat and all of its species while respecting the traditions and needs of nearby communities, which depend on the bay as a food source and for tourism revenue. Locals whose input was essential in the creation of the park, and who know the laws and regulations best, are the biggest stakeholders. Their continued cooperation and support of the park helps foster a network of education and choice, with the well-being of future generations in mind. It is hoped that, with the help and mutual commitment of the present and developing communities, all species—marine and human—will thrive in the coming years.

A Loreto Bay National Marine Park protected osprey feeds its chicks.

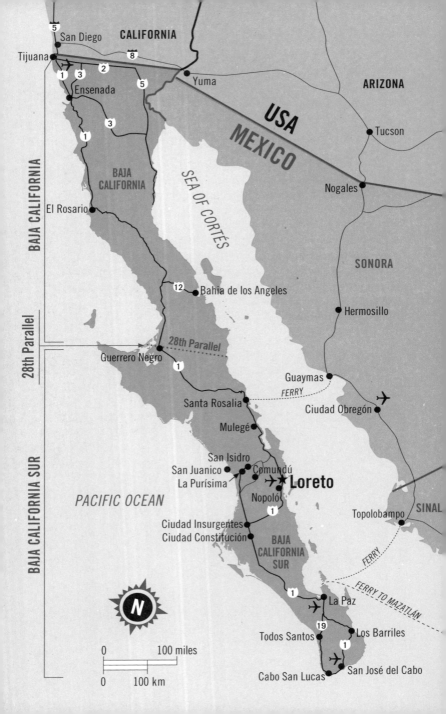

# 2

# Getting to Loreto
# and Getting Around

- Getting There
- Getting Around
- Where to Start

Photo by Alan Axelrod

Overview of Nopoló and Loreto

Baja California is made up of two of the thirty-one states of Mexico. The state of **Baja California Sur** (BCS) occupies the part of the peninsula south of the 28th parallel. It is bordered to the north by the state of **Baja California** (Norte), to the west by the Pacific Ocean, and to the east by the Gulf of California, also known as the Sea of Cortés. Loreto is located 225 miles (360 km) north of **La Paz**, the capital of BCS.

The state is known for its natural riches, and for its tourism. It includes the Pacific islands of **Natividad**, **Magdalena**, and **Santa Margarita**, as well as twelve islands in the Sea of Cortés, five of which are located directly offshore from Loreto. In 2003, the estimated population of BCS was 463,500. La Paz is Baja California's most populated city with 189,176 people. Although part of Baja California Sur, the east coast area from Loreto to Mulegé and up to Santa Rosalía is often called **mid-Baja**.

# GETTING THERE

Most Baja California guides start at the top of the peninsula and work their way down to Los Cabos, passing through Santa Rosalía, through Mulegé, into Loreto, and continuing on to La Paz. This book is written with Loreto as the focus, giving you a more complete picture of the town and surrounding area than any other source we know of. Keep in mind, while you are perusing these pages, that when you are looking at distances and directions, everything is relative to Loreto.

## By Plane

The airport, **Aeropuerto Internacional Loreto** (613-135-0565), is 1.8 miles (3 km) south of Loreto and 4.3 miles (7 km) north of the Nopoló area. It is small in relation to the growing tourist traffic in Loreto. There are a few facilities at the airport—a small bar in the main terminal area, a small bar and shop inside the departure lounge, and a small snack bar across the street. The airport has car rental agencies including Hertz, Budget, and Eurocar, as well as a taxi service.

### Aereo Calafia

Aereo Calafia has flights in and out of Loreto from both **Cabo San Lucas** and **Ciudad Obrégon** (on the mainland) on Tuesday, Thursday, and Saturday. Air charters and air taxi can also be arranged.

*Phone: 613-135-2503*
*Location: Hotel Plaza Loreto,*
  *Miguel Hidalgo*
*Web: aereocalafia.com.mx*

### Aeromexico

For financial reasons, Aeromexico ended a popular three-
times-per-week flight service
from San Diego in late 2006. We
understand that decision is under

Welcome to Loreto. Look for this historic bell in Loreto's central plaza.

review. Aeromexico still provides daily service to and from Loreto and
points in the United States through **Hermosillo**, across the Sea of Cortés
on the Mexican mainland.

*Phone: 613-135-0999; 800-237-663*
*Web: www.aeromexico.com*

### Alaska Airlines

At the time of this writing, Alaska Airlines has round-trip service
between Loreto and **Los Angeles** four times a week on Tuesday, Thursday, Friday, and Sunday.

*Phone: 1-800-ALASKAAIR (1-800-252-7522)*
*Hours: 5:00 a.m.–midnight (PST) (Daily)*
*Web: www.alaskaair.com*

### Continental Airlines

Continental Airlines began twice-weekly flights between George Bush
Intercontinental Airport in **Houston**, Texas, and Loreto, Mexico, the
airline's 31st Mexican destination, on June 7, 2007. Continental offers
service to more destinations in Mexico than any other U.S. airline.

*Phone: 800-523-3273*
*Web: www.continental.com*

### Delta Airlines

Delta Airlines began a daily round-trip service from **Los Angeles** to
Loreto on December 16, 2006.

*Phone: 800-221-1212*
*Web: www.delta.com*

## By Car

The **Mexican Federal Highway 1**, completed in 1973, transformed the accessibility of the Baja California region to tourism. Also called **Highway 1**, **Mexico 1**, or the **Transpeninsular Highway (Carretera Transpeninsular)**, it is the only paved road spanning the entire peninsula, running nearly 1,000 miles (1,609 km) from Ensenada in the north to Cabo San Lucas on the southern tip. Narrower than most American two-lane roads and often lacking a shoulder, Highway 1 is tricky to drive. Safety signs and guardrails are normally absent and drainage is often poor. During tropical storm "John" that passed over Loreto from the south in October 2006, the highway washed out in two places and people in Nopoló were cut off temporarily from the airport and from town. A new bridge is under construction over the **Río Loreto**, the main arroyo that cuts through town.

There are two basic safety rules for driving the highway—don't speed and don't drive at night. Also know that there are many sharp turns not protected with guardrails. Oncoming vehicles, especially large trucks, can make you feel uneasy in the narrow lanes with no shoulders. Cattle, burros, and goats are not fenced and are frequently spotted on the roads, especially at night where they lie on the roadway for warmth. Passing is common on straightaways; slow trucks and other vehicles will use their left-turn signal to tell you to pass when you feel comfortable and safe—not necessarily to signal that it is a good time to make a move.

On the stretch of road between Nopoló and Loreto, most people ignore the 60 kilometers per hour (37 mph) speed limit. However, there are police (sometimes with handheld radar), and they do pull people over. Have your vehicle registration and insurance paperwork ready just in case. The highway near Loreto will likely go from two lanes to four (or more) in the coming years, and signs of that widening project are evident from the grading along the roadway and the setbacks of light stanchions.

A word to the wise: The highway patrol in Baja California Sur, **Policía Federal de Caminos**, tend to be a little more vigilant than in other parts of Mexico. They do use radar extensively, and driving under the influence is a very serious offense.

Just north of Loreto, on the way to Mulegé, there is a **military checkpoint** in the northbound lane. You will be ordered to stop by a squad of Mexican soldiers bearing rifles and asked to step out of your car and open it for inspection. The young soldiers are generally courteous and polite, although serious, and will not cause you a problem provided you are not carrying illicit weapons or drugs. You can expect a ten- to thirty-minute delay, depending on traffic and time of day. North Americans are encouraged to not lose their cool here.

The highway is patrolled by the **Green Angels**. These trucks, loaded with tools and driven by mechanics, are here for tourists who have the misfortune of experiencing car problems while traveling in Mexico. Their help in getting you back on your way is free of charge and sponsored by the **Mexican Tourist Board**. Look for a deep-green pickup-style truck with a giant utility box on the back.

## By Ferry

The central Baja peninsula has connecting ferry service to and from the mainland as follows:

### La Paz–Mazatlán

The ferry runs from La Paz six days a week (or is it seven?—information varies as to weekend services), departing at 3:00 p.m. (15:00 hrs). The Wednesday ship is a cargo vessel, and only salon class is available for passengers. Other days all classes are available. Departs Mazatlán six (or seven) days a week at 3:00 p.m. (15:00 hrs). The Thursday ship is the same as the Wednesday ship out of La Paz. Travel time: about 19 hours.

### La Paz–Topolobampo

This route is serviced by Baja Ferries. Vehicles can be carried, but there is no general passenger traffic. Passenger traffic on the route is carried on a large catamaran which provides high-speed service between La Paz and Topolobampo. The boat does the round-trip in a day, taking about four hours for a crossing (35 knots). Both first and second classes are offered.

### Santa Rosalía–Guaymas

This route is being serviced twice a week by Sematur, with departures from Santa Rosalía on Tuesday and Friday at 10:00 p.m. (22:00 hrs).

For all pertinent up-to-date information, contact the ferries directly.

| *Baja Ferries* | *Sematur* |
|---|---|
| *Phone: 800-012-8770* | *Phone: 612-125-2366* |
| *Web: www.bajaferries.com* | *Web: www.bajaquest.com/faq/ferryservice.htm* |

# GETTING AROUND

## Car Rental

Loreto has Budget, Hertz, and Europcar car rental locations. Each has a small booth at the airport, while the main offices are in the town center.

### Budget Car Rental

Budget car rental will pick you up from the airport and provide you with competitively priced cars that include insurance, taxes, and free miles. The cars start at $70 per day for the smallest models, $140 per day for the nine-passenger Durango, and up to a 15-passenger van for $170 per day.

*Location: Av. Miguel Hidalgo at López Mateos*

*Phone: 613-135-1149 (Town); 613-135-0937 (Airport)*

*Hours: 8:00 a.m.–6:00 p.m.*

*E-mail: reservaloreto@budgetbaja.com*

### Europcar

Europcar's cheapest rental is $65 per day and includes insurance and free miles. They also have other models available for up to $120 per day. A representative will meet you at their airport booth and transport you to your car upon arrival.

*Location: Salvatierra and Independencia, Col. Centro*

*Hours: 8:00 a.m.–8:00 p.m.*

*Phone: 613-135-2260*

*Web: www.europcar.com.mx*

### Hertz

Hertz requires a driver's license and credit card, and all renters must be at least 25 years of age. Hertz offers rental cars either with or without insurance. The starting vehicle costs $30 per day without insurance, but $60 per day with all of the insurance. The most expensive car is the Suburban which is $120 without insurance and $160 with insurance. Hertz has a booth at the airport to get you to your car when you arrive.

*Location: On Callejon Romanitis; one block from the Malecón*

*off Av. Miguel Hidalgo, just around the corner from Budget*

*Hours: 7:30 a.m.–8:00 p.m.*

*Phone: 613-135-0800*

*E-mail: hertzloreto@hotmail.com*

## Taxis

There are two taxi companies in town, **Sitio Loreto** and **Sitio Juárez**. Both at the airport and from town, they generally charge a flat $15 to just about anywhere. Taxis can almost always be found parked on the north side of Avenida Miguel Hidalgo, just past the traffic light. They can also be found just north of the corner of Hidalgo and Francisco I. Madero around the corner from Mike's Bar.

*Hours: 6:00 a.m.–10:00 p.m. (Mon.–Thu.). Open 24 hours on weekends*

*Phone: 613-135-0434 (Sitio Loreto)*

*Phone: 613-135-0915 (Sitio Juárez)*

## Bus

The bus station is located in front of the baseball field and the children's park on **Calle Jaral** coming into town. **Aguila** and **ABC Lines** are stationed here. Buses to **La Paz** and **Los Cabos** are available throughout the day. La Paz departures are 8:00 a.m., 10:00 a.m., noon, 1:00 p.m., 2:00 p.m., 11:00 p.m. and midnight. Price is about $22 to La Paz. Comfortable air-conditioned buses with a movie included. Reservations recommended. Payment must be made within 24 hours of making a reservation. Locals tell us that the bus can also be used as a courier. They say it is faster and cheaper to put a package on the bus headed for Tijuana than it is to send by standard courier services.

*Hours: 7:00 a.m.–11:00 p.m. (Daily)*

*Phone: 613-135-0767*

# WHERE TO START

Decorated with handmade local arts and crafts and filled with information pamphlets, the tourist information office at the southeast corner of the **Palacio de Gobierno/City Hall** is a great place to start your visit to Loreto. The flyers, brochures, and maps give you basic lists of restaurants and activities in the area. More importantly, a visit here provides an opportunity to ask real people pertinent questions about any practical needs or services. The staff is friendly and happy to help you with specific concerns.

*Location: Corner of Salvatierra and Fco. I. Madero on the Zocalo (main square)*

*Hours: 8:00 a.m.–3:00 p.m. (Mon.–Fri.)*

*Phone: 613-135-0411*

Palacio de Gobierno/City Hall

La Misión Nuestra Señora de Loreto

**3**

# Major Attractions and Events

- The Mission
- The Museum
- The Malecón
- Festivals

## Nuestra Señora de Loreto

When Padre Eusebio Kino first arrived on the Baja peninsula, he attempted to establish a settlement and the first mission at what is now the modern-day site of San Bruno (just north of Loreto). The foundation and part of the walls still exist there. Why did San Bruno get abandoned and Loreto, instead, become the first mission of the Californias?

Although historians say the site was moved because of inadequate water supply, the locals have a different explanation. According to legend, on the first night ashore, the Spanish tied the figure of Nuestra Señora de Loreto on the back of a donkey. In the morning, they woke to discover the donkey and Nuestra Señora de Loreto were missing. They followed the donkey's tracks and eventually found Nuestra Señora de Loreto and brought her back to their camp. The next morning the same thing happened, and the missionaries found the donkey in the exact same place as the night before. They took it as a sign that this was the place for the virgin to remain—the place where she was "asking" to be. Nuestra Señora de Loreto has remained at the site of the current mission ever since. To locals, Nuestra Señora de Loreto is also known as "Reina y Patrona de las Baja California," (the "Queen and Patron of Baja California").

Much later, a lighter "traveler" version of the Nuestra Señora de Loreto figure was created. The tradition is that every year, a girl in town donates her hair to the mission, to be placed on "the traveler" (also known locally as "La Peregrina," "the Pilgrim"). The girl chosen is usually one who was sick and made a promise, a "manda," that if she would be healed she would cut off her hair when it was long enough and give it to Nuestra Señora de Loreto in return for her good health. Men occasionally donate their hair, too. The traveler, hair and all, can be seen just around the corner from the altar in its own small sanctuary in the mission.

"Traveler" version of the
Nuestra Señora de Loreto figure
Photo by Doug Ogle

From August 30 through September 7 Nuestra Señora de Loreto goes on a journey. Starting up at Rancho Las Parras on the road to San Javier, the "traveler" is taken in a procession to the Mission. The entire town turns out to greet her and the Loretanos walk with her as she is displayed to all of the citizens. On September 8, the actual Nuestra Señora de Loreto, in a re-creation of the landing of the first missionaries, is carried through town from the beach to the Mission.

# THE MISSION

The mission, **La Misión Nuestra Señora de Loreto**, is Loreto's number-one attraction. The inscription above the main entrance to the church reads "Cabeza y Madre de las Misiones de Baja y Alta California" ("Head and Mother of the Missions of Lower and Upper California"). The church, a simple building in the shape of a Greek cross, was built in the period 1704–1752. It suffered serious damage when the ceiling and bell tower collapsed during a hurricane in 1829, and was restored in 1976. The original statue of Nuestra Señora de Loreto, brought to shore by **Padre Kino** in 1667, is on display in the church's eighteenth-century gilded altar. It is respectful to remove your hat and speak quietly while inside. The store offers religious souvenirs.

*Location: On Salvatierra at Pino Suárez, across from the central square*

*Hours: 7:00 a.m.–8:00 p.m. (Daily); Store hours: 9:00 a.m.–1:00 p.m.,*
*    4:00 p.m.–6:00 p.m. (Mon.–Fri.)*

# THE MUSEUM

Built around 1769 as a commissary and warehouse next to the mission church, this annex was abandoned after the missionaries left Loreto. Over subsequent years, it served as a shelter, a prison, a primary school, a junior high school, and a boarding school for children from remote ranches and fishing villages of the region. Finally, the Federal government restored the building and opened it in 1973 as the **Museo de las Misiónes**.

The museum contains a small but interesting series of exhibits (in both Spanish and English) of historical, anthropological, and religious significance. It houses interesting artifacts and information about the indigenous tribes of the area, and their demise with the introduction of the European settlers' epidemic diseases. The museum also showcases remnants of eighteenth-century life, including tools, cooking implements, weapons, clothing, and religious art.

The museum is located adjacent to the church. Its shop sells a small assortment of Spanish-language books about the history, archaeology, and anthropology of Baja California with special emphasis on the missionary system. Admission is about $3.50.

*Location: Salvatierra No. 16, adjacent to the Mission*

*Hours: 9:00 a.m.–1:00 p.m. and 1:45 p.m.–6:00 p.m. (Tue.–Sun.)*

*Phone: 613-135-0441*

## THE MALECÓN

The Malecón, Loreto's waterfront promenade, and **Boulevard López Mateos** (the street that runs along it) comprise Loreto's best place to people-watch. Stroll along the Malecón in the afternoon to admire the beauty of the Sea of Cortés, Isla del Carmen, and Isla Coronado. Without many social options for locals, driving along the Malecón has become a staple of weekend nightlife. If you're lucky, there will be an open bench where you can sit and observe the hustle and bustle of true Loretano culture. The Malecón is also prime real estate for a few of Loreto's best restaurants and bars.

## FESTIVALS

There are two main festivals in Loreto each year: **El Día de la Virgin** and the **Fundación de la Ciudad** (the founding of the city). El Día de la Virgin, held September 5–8, is a fair to celebrate the Virgin of Loreto and Baja's first mission. Locals pull out all the stops for this holiday. Kids are told to save up for two big events every year: Christmas and El Día de la Virgin. The four-day-long party includes carnival rides, music, dancing, and plenty of beer. Experiencing this event is the perfect way to learn about Loreto and its people, not to mention having a great time parading along the Malecón.

From October 19–25, Loreto celebrates the city's founding in 1699 with the Fundación de la Ciudad festival. Along with music and dancing, the festival is known for the symbolic reenactment of the arrival of the Spanish missionaries. In it, a statue of Nuestra Señora de Loreto is taken out of the mission and out to sea, then ceremoniously brought back into Loreto as if it were the first time.

North of Loreto, in San Javier, the annual **San Francisco Javier Fair and Festival** takes place on December 3. Every year the almost deserted little village fills with people from the surrounding ranches to celebrate San Javier's birthday.

Locals and tourists alike enjoy strolling along the Malécon.
Photo by Doug Ogle

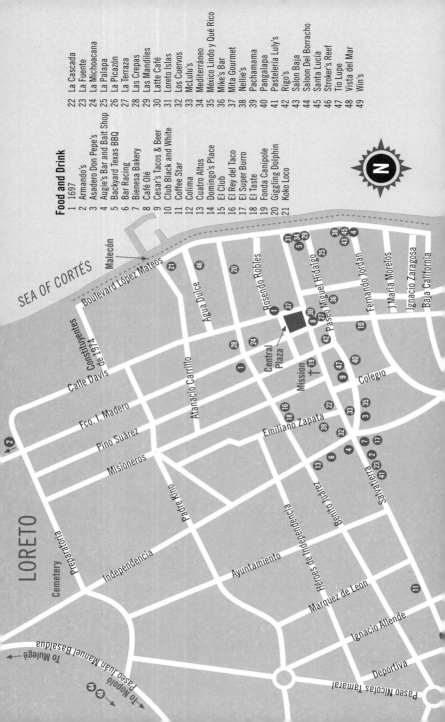

LORETO

**Food and Drink**

| | |
|---|---|
| 1 | 1697 |
| 2 | Armando's |
| 3 | Asadero Don Pepe's |
| 4 | Augie's Bar and Bait Shop |
| 5 | Backyard Texas BBQ |
| 6 | Bar Racing |
| 7 | Bienesa Bakery |
| 8 | Café Olé |
| 9 | Cesar's Tacos & Beer |
| 10 | Club Black and White |
| 11 | Coffee Star |
| 12 | Colima |
| 13 | Cuatro Altos |
| 14 | Domingo's Place |
| 15 | El Club |
| 16 | El Rey del Taco |
| 17 | El Super Burro |
| 18 | El Taste |
| 19 | Fonda Canipole |
| 20 | Giggling Dolphin |
| 21 | Koko Loco |

| | |
|---|---|
| 22 | La Cascada |
| 23 | La Fuente |
| 24 | La Michoacana |
| 25 | La Palapa |
| 26 | La Picazón |
| 27 | La Terraza |
| 28 | Las Crepas |
| 29 | Las Mandiles |
| 30 | Latte Café |
| 31 | Loreto Islas |
| 32 | Los Cuervos |
| 33 | McLulu's |
| 34 | Mediterráneo |
| 35 | México Lindo y Qué Rico |
| 36 | Mike's Bar |
| 37 | Mita Gourmet |
| 38 | Nellie's |
| 39 | Pachamama |
| 40 | Pangalapa |
| 41 | Pastelería Luly's |
| 42 | Rigo's |
| 43 | Salon Baja |
| 44 | Saloon Del Borracho |
| 45 | Santa Lucía |
| 46 | Stroker's Reef |
| 47 | Tio Lupe |
| 48 | Vista del Mar |
| 49 | Win's |

SEA OF CORTÉS

Malecón

Boulevard López Mateos

Constituyentes de 1914

Calle Davis

Fco. I. Madero

Pino Suárez

Misioneros

Cemetery

Preparatoria

Independencia

Padre Kino

Ayuntamiento

Héroes de Independencia

Benito Juárez

Marquez de Leon

Ignacio Allende

Deportiva

Paseo Nicolas Tamaral

To Nopolo
Paseo Juan Manuel Basdalua
To Mulegé

Agua Dulce

Rosendo Robles

Paseo Miguel Hidalgo

Fernando Jordan

J. Maria Morelos

Ignacio Zaragosa

Baja California

Atanacio Carrillo

Central Plaza

Mission

Emiliano Zapata

Colegio

Salvatierra

**4**

# Food and Drink

- Taco Stands
- Restaurants
- Sweets
- Refreshments
- Bars
- Clubs

⭐ **Addresses in Loreto**

Some street names in Loreto end with the suffix S/N for *sin número* (without number). The establishments on these streets do not have a numbered address. In fact, many establishments on streets with numbers don't have numbers either. In such cases we have done our best to orient readers by giving a cross street or other geographical reference to better help you locate what you are looking for. When possible and where appropriate we have included telephone numbers as well. As for hours of operation we have included those places formal enough to admit to regular hours.

# TACO STANDS

Finding a taco stand in Loreto is like finding a Starbucks in Seattle—they're everywhere, especially on the main drag, *Avenida Miguel Hidalgo*. Chances are, no matter where you eat your first taco, you will bite into it and declare that it is the best (and, for $1 to $1.50 per taco, the cheapest) taco you've ever had. We ate at every taco stand, and often, determined to answer the question "Who makes the best taco in Loreto?" To be honest, most of the tacos taste pretty much identical—that is, great. So we had to look at all the factors: not just flavor, but the freshness and quality of the ingredients, the subjective reaction to the first bite, the sizzle of the *carne* (meat), and the batter on the *pescado* (fish). Of course we took into account the overall "taco experience"—the ambiance, the speed and quality of service, and the surroundings. We know tacos. Here are our picks.

## Asadero Don Pepe's

*Meh...*

Only a few short blocks past the main traffic light on *Avenida Miguel Hidalgo*, Don Pepe's is a typical makeshift taco bar, complete with plastic tables and chairs. The seating area is unsightly and unrefined, but the friendly lady who works here will make you smile, and appreciates gringos who speak, or make an attempt to speak, Spanish. For a place that "specializes" in carne asada, these tacos were tasty but nothing out of the ordinary.

## Cesar's Tacos & Beer

*Our favorite*

Cesar's has the best *quesatacos* (tacos with cheese) in Loreto. Named after the owner's son, this friendly, newly remodeled restaurant on *Avenida Miguel Hidalgo* has excellent tacos, great guacamole, and a clean, quaint environment. You can choose to sit either under the shade of the straw palapa or in the sun, depending on your preference. There is a quick walk-up counter and plants lining the restaurant. Do not let the swarm of taco stands surrounding Cesar's on the main drag fool you, this place stands above the rest. On a scale of one to five, Cesar's gets seis stars!

*Hours: 9:00 a.m.–7:00 p.m. (Mon.–Sat.)*

## El Rey del Taco

*Size Matters*

Sit at the counter and talk to Paco, the King himself. El Rey is different from all the other taco joints because the tacos are significantly bigger here. Paco flurries around the kitchen and will have your tacos on a plate in minutes. If you're getting tired of carne, pescado, and *camarón* (shrimp), come here and try the "cabeza" tacos, made from the meat from a cow's head (brain not included). It's actually quite flavorful—and you can always ask to taste it before you commit to order. Of course, traditional ingredients are available and the fish tacos rival those from any other place in town. Look for the "Taco King" on *Benito Juárez at Misioneros*. It's literally a hole in the wall.

*Hours: 8:00 a.m.–2:00 p.m. (Wed.–Sun.)*

## McLulu's

*More Hype Than Flavor*

McLulu's is the original taco stand in Loreto, but twenty-five years of experience doesn't make it the best (just the most famous). McLulu's has what many other taco joints don't—flair, personality, and history. The tin roof, walls of faded stickers, and business cards of strangers past makes McLulu's the "surfer's" taco stand. McLulu's offers seven different kinds of tacos, but don't bother getting anything but the pescado at this typical coastal shack. Lourdes "Lulu" Armendáriz' slogan is "I'd rather be eating fish tacos at McLulu's." It is located on *Avenida Miguel Hidalgo*.

Photo by Doug Ogle

Pico de gallo is a condiment made from chopped tomato, onion, and chiles. Other ingredients such as lime juice, cilantro, cucumber. avocado, or radish may be added. Fresh salsa is better known as *salsa picada* (minced or chopped sauce), or *salsa mexicana* (the red tomatoes, white onions, and green chiles are the colors of the Mexican flag).

## Pangalapa

*Darn good*

Pangalapa sells mouthwatering and delicious tacos. Under a shady *palapa* (an open, thatched-roof patio), Pangalapa is surrounded by various plants and greenery and has a well-kept eating space. The tacos are served hot and sizzling right off the grill, and the accompanying tray of Mexican condiments includes sour cream, which is more rare than you'd expect. These are good tacos! A small counter in the back sells not only beer and *micheladas* (beer, salt, lime, and salsa, if you dare), but also breakfast (eggs, quesadillas, and omelets). The giant sign above the restaurant on *Avenida Miguel Hidalgo* is almost impossible to miss. High marks across the board!

## Rigo's

*Late-Night Delight*

Rigo's is one of the most popular places in town for a quick late night snack. They have bar-stool seating along *Avenida Miguel Hidalgo*, and serve great tacos and quesatacos. Plain and simple, Rigo's is a good taco place that is open late at night, closing anywhere from 8:00 p.m. to midnight (depending on the owner's mood) and the unpredictable hours are its claim to fame. Perfect for a quick refueling on a night out or for a before-bed snack.

# RESTAURANTS

For a town as small as Loreto, the number of restaurants and the overall quality of food is astoundingly good. Almost every place in town can be considered a seafood restaurant. You'll see a lot of clams and lobster, and a wide array of fish dishes on every menu that, because they are always so fresh, tend to wow customers. No matter where you eat, you should be prepared to pay in cash, as even the fancy restaurants that you'd expect to accept credit cards probably don't. This is likely to change in the very near future.

We've rated each eatery on a five-star basis (5 being the highest) for two categories: quality (⊙5) and price (⑤5). Quality not only includes the quality of the food, but also of the service, and the atmosphere—the overall eating experience. "5" for price means most expensive. The most expensive meals in Loreto typically range from $25 to $35 per person.

# *Breakfast*

## Café Olé  ⊙4  ⑤2

Café Olé is the place where you are most likely to run into someone you've previously met in Loreto. Known for its cheap but savory Mexican plates, locals and visitors congregate here for breakfast (although it is open for lunch and dinner, too). This iconic restaurant is the perfect spot to stay up to date on Loreto gossip while enjoying some huevos rancheros and a fresh fruit smoothie.

*Location: Just south of the main square on Fco. I. Madero*
*Hours: 7:00 a.m.–10:00 p.m. (Mon.–Sat.)*
*Phone: 613-135-0496*

## Santa Lucía ⭐5 💲2.5

For a mouthwatering yet healthy breakfast or lunch, Santa Lucía is your spot. During our stay in town, we were drawn back many times to Santa Lucía's breezy homestyle Mexican ambiance, friendly service, and reliably delicious meals. In the morning, fresh pastries are baked to perfection. We recommend you beat the breakfast rush if you want to get your hands on one of their famous whole-wheat cinnamon rolls. Santa Lucía also boasts healthy juice blends and some of the best coffee in town. Egg dishes can easily be prepared *sin llema* (without yolks) if you make the request. For lunch, you can't go wrong with the café's namesake sandwich, made with succulent chicken breast, avocado, and cheese on one of their home-baked whole-wheat baguettes. What's more, average prices range between only $3 and $6 per dish. One of our favorite spots got even better when it recently relocated two doors north on the Malecón, and it now has a bakery on the street front and a covered and uncovered second floor terrace overlooking the Sea of Cortés.

*Location: South end of the Malecón on Blvd. López Mateos*
*Hours: 6:30 a.m.–3:00 p.m. (Closed Wednesdays)*

Photo by Doug Ogle

# Lunch

## Armando's  ⊕2  ⑤2

Armando's Pizza is a run-of-the-mill pizza place whose main advantage is their wide variety of toppings. They do not sell pizza by the slice, but they can make you a pizza in twenty minutes. We advise you to place your order and then take a stroll while you wait. Small, medium, and large pizzas are available. Whatever your choice, you can easily fill up for less than $5 per person. Nothing special, but it is definitely close in quality to the pizza you get back home.

*Location: Salvatierra across from El Pescador*

*Hours: 11:00 a.m.–10:00 p.m.*

*Phone: 613-135-0245*

## Backyard Texas BBQ  ⊕3.5  ⑤4

From the owners of Mediterráneo and hidden in its shadow, comes this new bar and barbeque. Backyard's outdoor tables are each shaded by umbrellas, and by the back wall of the restaurant above it. Classic movies are projected onto this wall (7:00 p.m. to 11:00 p.m.) to entertain you as you sip one of the full bar's Mexican tap beers. On the food menu are $3 ribs, but with meat plates ranging from $13 to $30 dollars, this might be one of the more expensive barbecues you'll ever eat at. If you're desperate for some good ol' Texas-style cooking—smoked ham, barbecue chicken, pulled pork—come here, schmooze with the friendly staff, and be sure to take advantage of happy hour from 3:00 p.m. to 6:00 p.m.

*Location: At Mediterráneo on the Malecón, Av. Miguel Hidalgo*
*and Blvd. López Mateos*

*Hours: 2:00 p.m.–10:00 p.m. (Daily)*

## Colima  ⊕4.5  ⑤2.5

This bright and cheerful little place has arguably the best food in Loreto. Serving the full range of Mexican dishes for breakfast, lunch, or dinner, it is also the only "comida corrida" restaurant in Loreto. Comida corrida—literally "meal on the run" but more like a "daily special"—is very popular during the lunch hour here when the place can be packed from 1:00 p.m. to 3:00 p.m. Run by **Ulises and Jovine Flores** with their mother, **Evangelina**, doing the home cooking, this restaurant serves up delicious food using home-grown and imported spices from the Colima region of Mexico known for its culinary delights. It also boasts a satellite-connected large-screen TV and is air-conditioned too.

*Location: Benito Juárez just before Fco. I. Madero*

*Hours: 7:30 a.m.–10:00 p.m., (Tue.–Sat.); 7:30 a.m. –1:00 p.m. (Sun.)*

*Phone: 613-111-0853*

## Giggling Dolphin Restaurant and Boat Bar ⭐4 💲3

Opened in October 2006, the Giggling Dolphin Restaurant and Boat Bar has already established itself as a destination of choice. Conveniently located just one block from the marina, the menu of this open-air restaurant includes a wide variety of options (clams, shrimp, scallops, lobster, chicken, pork, steak, pasta, salads and soups), all delicious and all at reasonable prices. Owner **Uvaldo Islas Fernandez** created this fun and laid-back restaurant with an actual 1960 23-foot cabin cruiser bar. Treat yourself to a sustainable margarita. A what? You've got to see this pedal-powered blender, designed by Bruce Williams of the Dolphin Dive Center next door. An absolutely brilliant idea. The Giggling Dolphin is open until 10:00 p.m., so come for lunch or dinner. You won't be disappointed.

*Location: Benito Juárez between Davis and López Mateos*

  *(Next to Dolphin Dive Center)*

*Hours: noon–10:00 p.m. (Daily)*

*Phone: 613-109-9853 (Cell)*

## La Fuente ⭐1.5 💲3

La Fuente's claim to fame is its seating area, with its cobblestone floor and tables dressed in red cloth. Its central fountain gives it the feel of an outdoor courtyard, yet it is all enclosed so as to provide the comforts of indoor air-conditioning and quiet repose. The jamaica juice, served ice cold in a big pitcher, is the best thing on the menu.

*Location: Salvatierra No. 88*

*Hours: 7:00 a.m.–9:00 p.m.*

## Saloon Del Borracho ⭐4 💲1.5

This is a place that will appeal to a wide variety of people. On the one hand, it feels like an American bar, with two pool tables, neon beer signs, and a flat-screen TV. Yet at the same time, it serves up a great North American-style breakfast and lunch for the whole family. From its breakfast menu you can choose eggs, pancakes, waffles, or bagels and lox.

Enjoy a margarita made in a sustainable margarita blender at The Giggling Dolphin.

For lunch there is an assortment of deluxe burgers, barbeque chicken and ribs, fries, milkshakes, salads, chili, hot dogs, corn dogs, and a variety of sandwiches made to order. Try the chicken Caesar salad—literally a half head of romaine lightly grilled with chicken on top. This is a good place for a change of pace and the prices are great, with nothing on the menu costing more than $6.

*Location: Off the main highway about .3 mile (500 m) up the road toward San Javier*

*Season: Closed July through September.*

## Win's  ✪1.5  $2.5

Win's is a Mexican version of an American burger joint. However, the food is mediocre and the burgers are plain. The prices are reasonable but still more than any nearby taco stand. While Win's does not live up to its "best burgers in town" motto, it certainly works if you are getting sick of your taco-lunch routine. Win's offers two-for-one burgers on Wednesdays. Soft drinks and milkshakes are available.

*Location: Corner of Salvatierra and Independencia, next to El Pescador*

*Hours: 7:30 a.m.–10:00 p.m.*

Photo by Doug Ogle

## Dinner

### 1697 ✪4.5 ⑤3.5

A small but elegant menu graces one of the newest of Loreto's better restaurants. Proprietors **Kieran and Norma Raftery** are gracious hosts who take great pride in their small bistro and bar named for the year the mission was founded. Their menu primarily is made up of creatively prepared seafood. They will be expanding their fare to include some meat and chicken dishes soon. The desserts are sensational, too. They have the best flan in Loreto and their orange cake with cinnamon-sauce topping a la mode is worth a trip by itself. And last but not least, 1697 serves the best coffee in town. This place is a real gem.

*Location: Calle Davis No. 13 on the Central Square*
*Hours: 6:00 p.m.–10:00 p.m. (Tue.–Sun.)*
*Phone: 613-135-2538*

### Domingo's Place ✪3.5 ⑤4

One of oldest restaurants in town, Domingo's Place (formerly known as El Nido) has a tranquil, lush courtyard that, arguably, makes for the best ambiance in town. The place can get smoky from an open *chimenea* (a free-standing front-loading fireplace), however. Though primarily a steakhouse, we think the seafood here is equally impressive. You can't go wrong with a surf-and-turf. The service is top rate and prices are comparable to most other restaurants offering similar cuisine, with the mesquite-grilled steaks going for about $16. Any meat entree on the menu can be coupled with squid, shrimp, fish, or lobster for approximately $24. For a more casual experience, enjoy a drink and watch the game at the full bar. You will not leave disappointed, but you will leave with a full stomach.

*Location: Salvatierra No. 154*
*Hours: 2:00 p.m.–10:00 p.m.*
*Phone: 613-104-4016; Phone/Fax. 613-135-2445*
*E-mail: nidadomingo@hotmail.com*

### El Super Burro ✪3.5 ⑤2

Locals can judge how long you've been in Loreto by asking you whether you've been to El Super Burro yet. The "Super Donkey" burritos are famous for their size and taste. The house specialty, papas rellenas, a bottomless mixture of meat and potatoes that arrives in the same foil in

## Dining Tips

*Minstrels:* Bands of roving minstrels will often make the rounds of the town's better restaurants. They are actually quite good as both musicians and singers. The rule of thumb is that if you ask them to play, you leave them a tip. The going rate is $5 per song, which they will politely but firmly remind you about, should you try to pay less.

*Tipping:* Generally speaking, tipping follows the American pattern of leaving 15%–20% depending on the level of service.

Photo by Doug Ogle

which it was cooked, adds to the notoriety of the Super Donkey. El Super Burro, with all the characteristics of a taco stand, plus a variety of menu options bigger and better than the rest, has great reason to be a local favorite. Greasy, tasty, and open late. Come hungry or don't come at all.

*Location: Independencia, one block south of the traffic light off Salvatierra*

## El Taste  ✪3  $4.5

El Taste, "The Rib-Eye House," is one of the most expensive restaurants in Loreto. Take heed of its nickname and do not be led astray by the T-bone or filet. For $27, the rib eye is a tender cut of beef that comes to you on a sizzling hot plate. Its value, however, is questionable. Most steakhouses in Loreto offer similar cuts for around $16. The sleek interior, classy bar, friendly staff, and quality service are positives.

*Location: Benito Juárez and Emiliano Zapata*
*Hours: 8:00 a.m.–10:30 p.m.*
*Phone: 613-135-1489*

## Fonda Canipole  ✪5  $3.5

The bell tower of Loreto's mission overlooks this outdoor restaurant's stunning courtyard, home to one of the three original wells used to provide water for settlers. Authentically rustic and covered in traditional Mexican art and décor, you won't find an atmosphere like Canipole's anywhere else. The service is slow, but only because the friendly pro-pietaria, **Doña Sofia**, loves to chat with her guests and makes each of her homemade recipes from scratch on order. You can even watch her prepare them in her traditional outdoor kitchen. Appetizers go for an average of $4 and entrees are $6 to $10. Sofia charges substantially more for her daily specials because they are hard to come by and take longer to cook. Her *mole* (a classic Mexican sauce made with chiles and chocolate), for example, includes over thirty ingredients. In this relaxing setting, you might be tempted to order a shot of fine tequila or a fancy cocktail, but think twice. Drinks can easily end up costing you more than the food. Dinner here will last a few hours, a perfect way to acclimate to the relaxed Loreto lifestyle.

*Location: Pino Suárez No. 3, Col. Centro*
*Hours: 7:00 a.m.–1:00 p.m.; 4:30 p.m.–11:00 p.m.*
*Phone/Fax. 613-135-1886*

## La Cascada ✪3 💲3.5

The only restaurant on the historic, car-free section of Salvatierra west of the mission, La Cascada is a pleasant outdoor café with traditional Mexican food and lots of seafood. The menu's standout is Special Fish, which comes wrapped in foil and bursting with flavor. This Mexican eatery, open all day, offers good food, moderate prices, and a pleasant ambiance. It is also one of Loreto's few restaurants open on Sundays.

*Location: Corner Salvatierra and Emiliano Zapata*
*Hours: 8:00 a.m.–10:00 p.m (Thu.–Tue.)*

## La Palapa ✪3 💲3.5

A stone's throw away from the Malecón, La Palapa is a charming restaurant. The circular layout makes this a mariachi band's dream. A complimentary plate of chips, salsa, and guacamole is a nice touch—but the second one is on you. Portion sizes are fairly large and the food (especially the seafood) is satisfying, but nothing to write home about. Overall, the dimly lit La Palapa is a medium-priced casual restaurant, recommended for group dinners and cocktails. After dinner, keep the drinks coming at Mike's Bar a few doors down.

*Location: Av. Miguel Hidalgo between Blvd. López Mateos and Pipila*
*Hours: 1:00 p.m.–10:00 p.m.*
*Phone: 613-135-1101*

Sign at Fonda Canipole reads "Mole: Fragrant mixture of 34 ingredients combined at the right intensity, that conjure up the ancestral taste of our Earth!"

Photo by Doug Ogle

## La Terraza  ✪3.5  $3.5

La Terraza is located on a terrace above Café Ole. It is an ideal place to watch the sun setting over the historic buildings of Loreto. Make sure you are sitting on the edge of the terrace to maximize your view. There are a number of tasty seafood dishes similar to ones you would get at many restaurants in Loreto. Although there is nothing unique or special about the food at La Terraza, the view and the open-air atmosphere are incredible.

*Location: Fco. I. Madero (Above Café Olé)*
*Hours: 3:00 p.m.–11:00 p.m*
*Phone: 613-135-1846*

## Las Mandiles Restaurant and Bar  ✪2.5  $2.5

Newly located on the Malecón next to Mediterráneo, Las Mandiles offers Mexican fare and, of course, beer. Its hook is the live rock 'n' roll band that plays in the evening.

*Location: On the Malecón next to Mediterráneo*
*Hours: 4:00 p.m.–1:00 a.m. (Daily)*

## Loreto Islas  ✪4.5  $2.5

This clean, bright, air-conditioned restaurant specializes in seafood. Islas runs on a fish-of-the-day program, serving only one type of fish each day (although it is usually their fresh sea bass). How would you like Islas to prepare your fish? Almost any way will cost just under $10. Their specialty preparations include garlic butter, a Meunier-and-orange glaze, or an almond sauce, all of which come in generous portions. The restaurant also doubles as an art gallery, with paintings of the Loreto area gracing the walls. We recommend Loreto Islas if you want some of the best fish in town and a pleasant dining atmosphere. Loreto Islas also serves one of the best breakfasts in town.

*Location: Blvd. López Mateos on the Malecón*
*Hours: 8:00 a.m.–9:00 p.m.*
*Phone: 613-135-2341*
*Web: www.palmarojagallery.com/restaurant.php*

## Los Cuervos  ◎2  ⑤2

Los Cuervos is a run-of-the-mill Mexican restaurant, serving reasonably priced national classics of inconsistent quality. Rarely visited by tourists, the restaurant is not enticing, yet it is plenty accommodating. It has a down-home feel that may appeal to those in search of an alternative to Loreto's other tried-and-true lunch spots.

*Location: Salvatierra*

*Hours: 10:00 a.m.–1:00 a.m. (Mon.–Sat.); 10:00 a.m.–8:00 p.m. (Sun.)*

*Phone: 613-113-3364*

## Mediterráneo  ◎4  ⑤4.5

Mediterráneo's expansive balcony offers a spectacular view of the sea and is a great place to gather to eat and drink and enjoy the scenery. Gracious hosts **Lee and Carol Boyd** have created a Mediterranean-style menu offering seafood plates, meat, pizza, and pasta dishes, and boasting a lengthy wine list. The service and the food are excellent. It is a large restaurant and, so far, it is easy to get a table for lunch or dinner. They will serve large parties and it is best to call ahead so they can set up properly.

*Location: Corner Blvd. López Mateos and Av. Miguel Hidalgo*

*Hours: 12:30 p.m.–4:30 p.m (Lunch); 6:00 p.m.–10:00 p.m. (Dinner)*

*Phone: 613-135-2571*

*Web: www.mediterraneo-loreto.com*

## México Lindo y Qué Rico  ◎2  ⑤3

The easy-to-miss gated archway on the south side of Avenida Miguel Hidalgo leads into the green courtyard of México Lindo, a simple restaurant offering basic takes on the traditional Mexican dishes. The covered outdoor terrace is decorated with hanging plants, kitschy relics of Loreto's past, and a birdcage with active and colorful species.

*Location: Av. Miguel Hidalgo*

*Hours: 8:00 a.m.–10:00 p.m.*

*Phone: 613-135-1175*

## Mita Gourmet ✪4.5 ⑤3.5

Whether you pass an afternoon wining and dining on mouthwatering seafood dishes, or spend an evening immersed in the beauty of the historic town center, any time is a good time to be at Mita Gourmet. The restaurant is almost entirely outdoors, with a covered seating area facing out on the cobblestone square. A satellite-equipped TV resting in an enclosed box outside entertains kids while you enjoy the overhanging trees and tranquil atmosphere. (The TV is turned on mostly in the daytime, usually by request.) Just beyond your table is a fountain and a beautiful gazebo in the main square, with the historic mission as the backdrop. We found everything on the menu to be delicious, but if you still can't decide, the friendly proprietors, **Martha and JuanCarlos Cortés**, will be more than happy to steer you in the right direction. Don't miss their specialty, chocolate clams ("chocolate" being the color of the clams); you simply cannot leave Loreto without trying a plate or two of these. An amazing value, it is the most economical high-end restaurant in town. No trip to Loreto is complete without a stop at Mita Gourmet.

*Location: Calle Davis No. 13; Centro Histórico*
*Hours: 11:00 a.m.–11:00 p.m. (Mon.–Sat.)*
*Phone: 613-135-2025*
*E-mail: mitagourmet@yahoo.com.mx*

## Nellie's Tapas and Sushi Bar ✪4 ⑤2.5

Nellie's rooftop tapas bar is the place to go for stunning views of the Sea of Cortés. It is fast becoming another go-to place in Loreto, featuring delicious tapas, premium liquors, and rave-worthy sushi. Chef **Edgar**

Photo by Doug Ogle

**San Pancho** trained in Japan under a sushi master for five years, and you'll be able to taste his proficiency in his delicious sushi combinations. Ask for Nellie's special roll, tempura shrimp stuffed with crabmeat and roe on greens with one of Edgar's delectable original sauce creations. A meeting place for the local cognoscenti.

*Location: Above BajaBOSS on the Malecón, between Jordán and Paseo Hidalgo*
*Hours: 4:00 p.m.–10:00 p.m. (Wed.–Sun.)*

## Pachamama ✪4.5 ⑤4

Pachamama (which means Mother Earth) is an ideal dinner destination. Located on a pleasant, simple side street, the restaurant provides a peaceful dining experience, complete with tiki torches and soft background music. It is an open-air restaurant and offers an array of high-class dishes. Particularly of note are the appetizers and complimentary bread, which comes steaming hot with a signature oregano-and-olive-oil dip. The menu has a wide range of salads and meat entrees. Everything tastes terrific so you simply cannot go wrong. Our recommendation is the New York Strip steak, a high quality, tasty cut of beef at a very reasonable price. Mother Earth gives you your money's worth!

*Location: Emiliano Zapata No. 3, Centro Histórico*
*Hours: 5:00 p.m.–10:00 p.m. (Wed.–Mon.)*
*Phone: 613-135-2219*
*E-mail: pachamama@prodigy.net.mx*

## Tío Lupe ✪4.5 ⑤3.5

In the heart of town on Avenida Miguel Hidalgo, you might walk past Tío Lupe without even noticing it. Once you're inside, though, it will be hard to leave. It is one of our favorites. The roomy dining area provides a breezy atmosphere, best described as a three-walled barn with a high, thatched roof. In addition to its indoor-outdoor dining environment, the hanging plants and decorative wall murals make Tío Lupe at once both upbeat and relaxing. A complimentary serving of homemade scallion dip whets the appetite for the rest of the menu. We recommend the *queso fundido* (spicy melted cheese and sausage), the fish *à la Castro Ruiz* (white-wine-and-cheese sauce), or any of the seafood specials—particularly shrimp and lobster—but you also can't go wrong with any of the cheaper, traditional Mexican plates. Attention, fishermen: if you bring in your catch, Tío Lupe will prepare it for a modest cost. Indeed, Tío Lupe provides quite a meal, with excellent service to match. Although not fancy, this restaurant is a hidden gem, and a *Best Guide* favorite.

*Location: Av. Miguel Hidalgo and Colegio*

*Hours: 8:00 a.m.–10:00 p.m.*

*Phone: 613-135-1882*

*Web: www.eltioluperestaurant.com*

## To the North

### La Picazón  ❂5  ⑤4

Finding La Picazón is almost as thrilling as eating there. The isolated, "secret" beach hideaway, run by gracious hosts **Alejandro and Imelda Igartua** and their sons, is worth the 3.7-mile (6-km) dirt-road drive that parallels the beach north of town, with gourmet food meriting high marks across the board. Everything from the wraps to the seafood plates and the quesadillas to the hamburgers is sure to satisfy diners, in both quality and quantity. The dining area sits along the beautiful secluded beach, directly across from **Isla Coronado**, which is why many diners arrive by sea. La Picazón is also a great spot to have your catch of the day prepared. If you are looking for something to spice up your afternoon, a trip to La Picazón is like finding the prize at the end of a scavenger hunt.

Drive north along the Malecón and follow the road as it turns left. Take your first right onto Calle Davis, a paved road that turns into dirt two blocks later, just past La Pinta Hotel. Now the adventure begins.

The view from La Picazón

Follow this dirt road for approximately 3.7 miles (6 km). At times, the road splits and you may be confused as to which way to proceed, but small signs continually mark the way so if you just keep heading north you shouldn't get lost. Just when you are convinced the road is too bumpy or that you've made a wrong turn, you should see the first blue sign for La Picazón. The signs will eventually lead you to a tall white house with an adjacent palapa—and, most likely, plenty of cars parked outside.

*Location: Beachfront north of town*
*Hours: noon–5:00 p.m. (Tue.–Sat.)*
*Phone: 613-109-9029*
*E-mail: lapicazon@hotmail.com*

## *To the South*

### Vista del Mar ⭐4 💲3

Despite the limitations of its name, Vista del Mar (View of the Sea) offers a stunning view of both the Sea of Cortés and the Sierra de la Giganta behind it—and a mean plate of clams. Six dollars will buy you a plate stacked with chocolate clams, a large and succulent local delicacy. Its seaside perch emphasizes that any seafood dish ordered here is sure to be fresh. Vista del Mar is well worth the extra drive south. Don't forget to peer through the restaurant's giant, ground-mounted binoculars to examine every bluff and ridge of the mountains in the distance.

*Location: Just a mile south of Nopoló, the only stop on Highway 1 before*
  *Puerto Escondido*
*Hours: 9:00 a.m.–8:00 p.m.*

Photo by Sara Axelrod

# SWEETS

## Bienesa Bakery

The main bakery in town, Bienesa has doughnuts, buns, cakes, cookies, rolls, and more. Its low prices are indicative of the quality of its goods, which in our experience were neither particularly fresh nor tasty. That being said, Bienesa is the only place in town to get certain types of baked goods (save for Santa Lucía, whose select but top-notch pastries usually sell out by mid-morning). In the rare event that you arrive just after a fresh batch of goodies comes out of the oven, you may be pleasantly surprised.

*Location: On Salvatierra across from El Pescador, just before the traffic light*
*Hours: 9:00 a.m.–9:00 p.m.*

## Las Crepas

The only crepería in Loreto, Las Crepas is owned and run by a Frenchman who moved to Loreto with a desire to introduce the town to authentic French cuisine. The crepes are very reasonably priced and large, regardless of whether you get a savory or sweet crepe. They also have homemade cakes, quiches, tarts, coffee, frappés, and juices. The menu includes all of the classic crepes, including ham and cheese, Nutella and banana, jam, and most anything else you would want. Great freshly-made authentic French crepes—what more do you need to know?

*Location: Benito Juárez, two blocks from the Malecón*
*Hours: 9:00 a.m.–9:00 p.m. (Tue.–Sun.)*
*Phone: 613-113-4846*

## Pastelería Luly's

Located in a house set back off Salvatierra across the street and just north of El Pescador, Pastelería Luly's is a small catering business which is known for proprietress Luly's cakes (especially wedding cakes) and other event pastries. Although not a retail establishment, the local community knows her well and she speaks English.

*Location: Salvatierra, just north of Independencia*
*Phone: 613-135-0219*

# REFRESHMENTS

## Coffee Star

Caffeine addicts are likely to find Coffee Star, a Loretan Starbucks look-alike, to be a suitable fix for their morning cravings. Don't let its looks fool you, however. Just because the sign on the door is green doesn't mean the barista won't look at you strangely when you ask for a triple tall nonfat sugar-free vanilla and hazelnut latte with whipped cream. Our recommendation? When it comes to ordering, stick to the basics. Pastries too.

*Location: On Salvatierra at Ignacio Allende*

*Hours: 8:00 a.m.–8:00 p.m (Mon.–Sat.); 1:00 p.m–8:00 p.m. (Sun.)*

## La Michoacana

Refreshment central Michoacana is the go-to place for a cold, sweet treat. This oasis should not be missed. A cooler at the front of the store holds icy vats filled with different flavors of fresh juice. The locals' secret blend is a mix of a sweet jamaica juice (from the hibiscus flower) and fresh-squeezed lemonade. To order it, ask for "jamaica (ha-MY-kah) y limón." Beyond the juices, large freezers hold homemade popsicles in a rainbow of fresh fruit flavors, both basic and tropical, with and without cream, none costing more than $1.50. Finally, in the back of the store you'll find the finest ice cream in town, with everything from fruit gelati to traditional chocolate-chip ice cream. Yum!

*Location: On Fco. I. Madero just south of Benito Juárez*

*Hours: 8:00 a.m.–midnight*

La Michoacana has freezers filled with ice cream and homemade popsickles and ice cream bars.

## Latte Café

This brand new coffee and dessert shop which opened August 2007 is owned and operated by the owners of Café Olé next door on Francisco I. Madero. It has indoor and outdoor seating and a couple of Internet terminals for use as well.

*Location: Just south of the main square on Fco. I. Madero*

*Hours: 7:00 a.m.–10:00 p.m. (Mon.-Sat.)*

*Phone: 613-135-0496*

# BARS

### Augie's Bar and Bait Shop

Those who walk into Augie's in search of fishing bait will all leave empty-handed. The "bait" in the name "Augie's Bar and Bait Shop" refers to the female bartenders used to lure in customers. What its name fails to reveal is that Augie's is one of Loreto's top sports bars. The bar has lots of sports channels and enough different screens to watch them all at once. Although Augie's is big with the gringo crowd, beer does not discriminate—everyone is welcome here. Don't be surprised to walk into Augie's at 10:00 a.m. and see a group of guys puffing cigars and going to work on a round of Coronas.

*Location: Blvd. López Mateos*

*Hours: 8:00 a.m.–10:00 p.m.*

### Bar Racing

Racing is an open-air bar with occasional dancing and live music. There are a few different seating areas, making it a decent place to have a drink with friends, chat, and relax. Don't count on Racing for any stimulus besides alcohol. It would be a fun place to go if it was crowded, but it never seems to be, because everyone is at Koko Loco instead. At least it stays open late!

*Location: On Calle Independencia*

*Hours: 6:00 p.m.–midnight (Mon.-Thu.); 9:00 p.m.–4:00 a.m. (Fri. & Sat.)*

## Cuatro Altos

Cuatro Altos is named for the four-way stop at the intersection where it is located, the cross streets of Benito Juárez and Independencia. The restaurant is upstairs in the complex, and is well equipped with a large flat-screen TV. The ceiling and walls are rustically decorated with bones and stuffed blowfish, giving the place an old-fashioned feel. The lunch and dinner menu is as simple as it gets, ranging from basic seafood dishes ($8 to $11) to hamburgers, nachos, and hot wings (all $5). The real appeal of Cuatro Altos, however, is its full bar. One of the best in town, the bar is a great place to sit and enjoy a margarita or two. A sushi bar will be opening soon on the bottom floor.

*Location: Corner Benito Juárez and Independencia*
*Hours: 11:00 a.m.–3:00 p.m. (Lunch); 6:00 p.m.–11:00 p.m (Dinner)*

## Mike's Bar

Why is Mike's *the* bar in Loreto? Some might credit the fact that it is one of the original establishments in Loreto and has been around for over twenty years. Others may cite rumors of famous explorers and writers like John Steinbeck who stopped in for a drink in decades past. But there may be no reason as to how and why Mike's became "the spot" other than the recognized need for Loreto to have "a spot" and the unspoken consensus that Mike's would be it. It is special because is isn't anything special—just a small room with one long curving counter occupied by either a flock of inebriated tourists, a set of sunburned fishermen,

Photo by Doug Ogle

the mariachi band you bought a song from at dinner, or all of the above. If you are not impressed the first time you visit, look up. You will see a giant whale bone hung from the ceiling. If you are still not impressed, have a few more cocktails and pretend you are, because Mike's is the best bar in town, and no one leaves until it closes at 3:00 a.m.

*Location: On the corner of Av. Miguel Hidalgo and Fco. I. Madero*
*Hours: noon–3:00 a.m.*

## Stroker's Reef

Motorcycle lovers will appreciate this laid-back new bar, decked out in Harley Davidson décor, resting on a quiet street a half block from Loreto's waterfront promenade. Stroker's has a pool table in great condition, a TV, and most importantly, air-conditioning. You might be hard pressed to find this bar filled to capacity, unless you bring enough biker buddies to fill it. Happy hour is from 3:00 p.m. to 8:00 p.m.

*Location: To get to Stroker's Reef, follow the Malecón north; you'll see a sign.*
*Hours: 3:00 p.m.–11:00 p.m. (Mon.–Sat.)*

# CLUBS

## Club Black and White

This new disco and karaoke club is a welcomed addition to the Loreto nightlife scene. Up-and-coming rival to larger, breezier Koco Loco, the club is crammed into a small space, and can get hot, but that's the way locals seem to like it on Saturday night into the wee hours. The black and white theme is catchy, but doesn't really add much to the clubbing experience—it's quite dark in there. Nonetheless, there is a disco ball, and who doesn't like a hearty Mexican tequila-induced karaoke session every now and then? Shots sell for $4 to $6 dollars at the inconspicuous corner bar.

*Location: Fco. I. Madero just north of Miguel Hidalgo*
*Hours: 9:00 p.m.–2:00 a.m. (Fri.); 10:00 p.m.–4:00 a.m. (Sat.)*
*Cover charge: $5*

## El Club

Winning the prize for best name of any venue in Loreto, El Club is Loreto's version of a classy strip club. Sit right beside the stage, smoke a cigar, drink a Tecate and enjoy the show. Since El Club makes most of its money on drinks, expect to be asked multiple times if you'd like another. Dancers go topless, but not completely nude (the same rules may or may not apply for private dances—you'll have to explore that on your own). Since the peso equivalent of a U.S. dollar is approximately a 10 peso coin, and coins don't exactly suffice for this type of venue (tip-wise), you are encouraged to exchange your real money for "Club Dollars." We don't know where these yellow pieces of paper have been, but we noticed they are stamped on the back at every use, which naturally leads to the entertaining game of seeing who has the dollar with the most stamps on it. A visit to El Club is surely a fun time, but you might want to wash your hands on the way out.

*Location: Entering town from the highway, hang your first right at the roundabout at Paseo Nicolas Tamaral, heading south.*
*Hours: 3:00 p.m. until closing (Fri. & Sat.)*

## Koko Loco

Koko Loco is the only true dance club in Loreto. If you're looking to go out on a Saturday night, there's no competition. Koko Loco is known for its eclectic patronage, including local Mexican teenagers, older couples (the teens' parents), bosses, employees, tourists, and fishermen. You'll find them all here. The dance floor can get so crowded it may overflow into the seating area, which may overflow onto the two balconies, which never seem to overflow. Drinks are pricier than in restaurants; beers run about $2.50 each. If you are ready to dance you shouldn't have a problem getting in, although technically you have to be age 18 to enter. Once you do, you're bound to have fun.

*Location: On the Malecón across from the marina*
*Hours: Fri. and Sat. night (Best on Sat., after midnight)*
*Cover charge: $5*

## Salon Baja

Spring-break–loving college partygoers will enjoy this large, outdoor nightclub, where all drinks are served in liters, providing cheap alcohol in quantity. With lots of open space itching to be filled, Salon Baja has the potential to become one of Loreto's biggest party venues. Liters of beer cost $6 except on Fridays when, for a $20 cover fee, you can drink 'til you drop—a dangerously appealing deal. Salon Baja's motto is "litros y burritos." We are confident you'll get both in excess here. Salon Baja is expecting to expand soon with the addition of a large pool and terrace.

*Location: Blvd. López Mateos and Fernando Jordán, between Augie's and BajaBOSS; behind Santa Lucía*
*E-mail: pierrer@salonbaja.com.mx*
*Web: www.Salonbaja.com.mx*

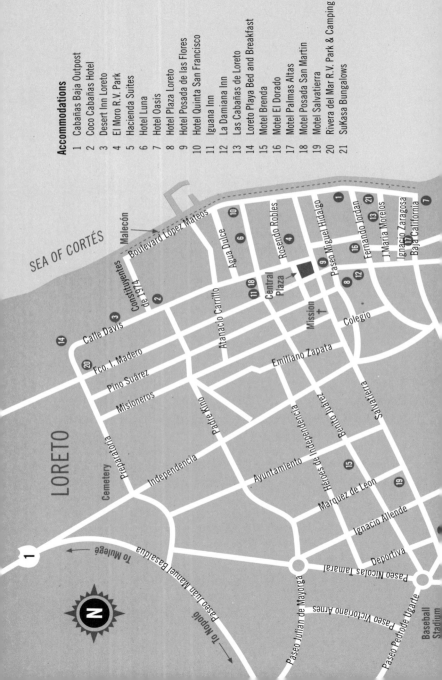

# LORETO

**SEA OF CORTÉS**

## Accommodations

1 Cabañas Baja Outpost
2 Coco Cabañas Hotel
3 Desert Inn Loreto
4 El Moro R.V. Park
5 Hacienda Suites
6 Hotel Luna
7 Hotel Oasis
8 Hotel Plaza Loreto
9 Hotel Posada de las Flores
10 Hotel Quinta San Francisco
11 Iguana Inn
12 La Damiana Inn
13 Las Cabañas de Loreto
14 Loreto Playa Bed and Breakfast
15 Motel Brenda
16 Motel El Dorado
17 Motel Palmas Altas
18 Motel Posada San Martin
19 Motel Salvatierra
20 Rivera del Mar R.V. Park & Camping
21 SuKasa Bungalows

**5**

# Accommodations

- Super-Cheap
- Budget
- Moderate
- High End
- Bed and Breakfast
- R.V. Parks

# SUPER-CHEAP

## Motel Brenda

Located in a non-tourist area on the outskirts of town, Motel Brenda works fine as a place to grab a bed for the night, but offers little more. With thirteen doubles, and two two-bed suites, odds are there will be a vacancy on any given night. Prices are based on the number of people per room: $23 for one person, $26 for two, and $29 for three. Key and remote control deposits are $5 each. Rooms are all air-conditioned with a TV, and are relatively clean and well kept. Certainly not the nicest place to stay and not a great location, but it is an efficient and cheap shelter for a night.

*Location: Benito Juárez and Marqués de León*

## Motel Posada San Martin

The accommodations here are as basic as it gets. The rooms go for $25 per night, and provide a bed barely big enough for two, a chair, and nothing more. Every room comes with air-conditioning, so if you do not mind the poor location and the meager rooms then this will work as a cheap place for a bed.

*Location: Benito Juárez and Fco. I. Madero*

*Phone: 613-135-1107*

## Motel Salvatierra

One of the cheapest accommodations available in Loreto, this simple motel is on the outskirts of town near the main highway. Rooms range in size from singles to cramped five-person units, and range in price from $24 to $34 per night. All rooms have air-conditioning, color cable TV, a bed, and a toilet, and that is about it. A great deal for a group looking for an extremely cheap night's rest, as long as they don't mind being slightly overcrowded.

*Location: On Salvatierra across from the PEMEX gas station*

*Phone: 613-135-0021*

# BUDGET

## Hotel Quinta San Francisco

Hotel Quinta San Francisco is located on the Malecón looking out over the Sea of Cortés. There are four doubles at $50 per night, and two family rooms which go for $55 per night. Every room is air-conditioned. A great location and the small size gives it a friendly, guest-house feel.

*Location: Just past Benito Juárez on Blvd. López Mateo (Malecón)*

## Motel El Dorado

Motel El Dorado is the newest motel in town and has eleven new rooms as well as a nice sports bar on the property. Specializing in sport fishing, Motel El Dorado is just a couple of blocks from the water, and offers fishing charters for good prices directly through the hotel. Singles are $45 and doubles cost $50. All rooms have air-conditioning and cable TV, and the hotel has phone, fax, Internet, and laundry services. The decent location and good prices as well as a terrific setup for private *panga* (small sport-fishing boat) charters makes it a go-to spot for a fishing trip to Loreto.

*Location: Miguel Hidalgo and Pipila*
*Phone: 613-135-1500; Fax: 613-135-1700; Toll Free: 888-314-9023*
*Web: www.moteleldorado.com*
*E-mail: info@moteleldorado.com*

## Motel Palmas Altas

Motel Palmas Altas is a budget accommodation short on charm that sits down a dirt road and offers little in the way of amenities. It has twenty-four rooms, ranging in price from $22 to $45 per night, and also has an individual unit with a kitchen available for $50 per night. Every room comes with air-conditioning and the property has a small pool. This is a decent option for travelers on a tight budget.

*Location: Blvd. López Mateos*
*Phone: 613-135-1353*

Photo by Doug Ogle

Sit on a bench along the Malecón and relax while watching pelicans, a common sight.

# MODERATE

### Cabañas Baja Outpost

Baja Outpost is a unique institution in the Loreto area. It is designed to be an all-inclusive resort destination and specializes in offering every recreational activity directly through the hotel itself. Baja Outpost offers scuba diving, snorkeling, whale watching, kayaking, mountain biking, cave painting tours, town tours, and island tours. Special deals can be arranged ahead of time, combining activities and accommodations for reduced prices. Based on the nature of the establishment, it is wise to always call ahead of time to arrange the exact package you want. There is nothing special about the accommodations., but it is a terrific solution if you want an easy, no-hassle way to fully experience ecotourism on the Baja peninsula.

*Location: Blvd. López Mateos*

*Phone: 1-888-649-5951 (U.S. toll free); 52-613-135-1134 (International)*

*E-mail: out@bajaoutpost.com*

*Web: www.bajaoutpost.com*

## Coco Cabañas Hotel

Coco Cabañas is an extremely popular hotel on Calle Davis, around the corner from the marina, just one block from the Sea of Cortés and a short walk from Loreto's central shopping area. There are eight separate cabañas for one to three people, each with a kitchen and dining area, air-conditioning, TV, bathroom, and shaded porch. The central landscaped courtyard has a pool and many plastic beach chairs and umbrellas. This is a great place to relax and schmooze with the other guests after a day out—a day that the accommodating proprietor, Barrett Scalapino, will be glad to help you plan. The daily rate is $70 per night or $420 per week. Visit their website for photos.

*Location: Calle Davis*
*Phone: 613-135-1729*
*E-mail: Barrett@coco-cabanas.com*
*Web: www.cococabanasloreto.com*

## Hacienda Suites

Hacienda Suites is a newly constructed hotel located on the edge of town, across from the bus station and a bit farther away from the water than its competitors. The hotel closely resembles the traditional Mexican hacienda architectural style. The rooms wrap around a central courtyard, complete with a pool, and Hacienda's very own bar, **La Molienda** and restaurant, **Rancho Viejo**. Every Saturday, starting at 7:30 p.m., the courtyard hosts **"Fiesta Mexicana,"** an event for all guests, with traditional Mexican food, song, and dance. Standard suites are $79, Junior suites are $95 (rarely available), and Master suites start at $115. The premises are clean and all rooms are big enough for two adults and two children, with an extra $12 per night for an additional person. Every room is air-conditioned and comes with a 21-inch TV, along with a bathroom and telephone. There is laundry service, room service, and concierge service.

*Location: Salvatierra #152, just west of the PEMEX station*
*Phone: 1-866-207-8732 (in USA), 1-800-224-3632 (in Mexico); Fax: 613-135-0202*
*E-mail: info@haciendasuites.com*
*Web: www.haciendasuites.com*

## Hotel Luna

The family-operated Hotel Luna is a new hotel in Loreto, with only three rooms. The friendly, multilingual hosts keep the modern rooms clean, cool, and well-equipped with air-conditioning, cable television, and wireless internet. Extremely close to the beach, Hotel Luna is a quiet retreat, conveniently located next door to a quality restaurant, the Giggling Dolphin. On the top of the hotel is **Bar Eclipse**, offering great views of the mountains and the sea, a 42" TV, and Italian espresso maker—certainly a nice place to relax and enjoy a drink. A two-person room goes for $60.

*Location: Calle Benito Juárez between Blvd. López Mateos and Calle Davis*
*Hours: Bar Eclipse open 7:00–midnight (Sun., Tue.); 7:00 p.m.–1:00 a.m. (Fri., Sat.)*
*Web: www.hotellunaloreto.com*

## Hotel Oasis

Located at the very southern end of the Malecón, Hotel Oasis has a long beachfront property that boasts of having top-class hospitality services. Primarily known as a fishing base, Oasis has its own private fleet of fishing boats and can offer you deals on fishing trips. Oasis is a family-run hotel, and most guests feel right at home. There are forty large air-conditioned rooms, each with a private balcony or patio, closet space, bathroom, TV, coffee maker, and double beds. Rooms start at $70 and go up to $170 depending on the size, quality, and location. The rooms are outdated, starkly decorated, and a little funky, but the friendly maids keep them quite clean and comfortable. There is a large heated pool and bar/lounge area in the courtyard. The patio restaurant opens at 5:00 a.m. daily so that you can grab a hearty breakfast before you head out for your fishing excursion. Generally, the food is highly praised, but the quality is said to have declined in recent years. The Oasis caters to fishermen and therefore is popular among Loreto old-timers. Hotel Oasis is in a great location, and with plenty of shade and hammocks, it's a very laid-back, relaxing place to stay, and a decent value.

*Location: López Mateos and Calle Baja California, at the south end of*
    *the Malecón*
*Phone: 613-135-0211 and 613-135-0112*
*Web: www.hoteloasis.com*

Photo by Doug Ogle

Mobile street vendor

5

ACCOMMODATIONS

## Hotel Plaza Loreto

Hotel Plaza Loreto is a relatively inexpensive option in a terrific central location, only one block away from the mission and the Loreto historic center and three blocks away from the water. It is well kept and has a nice central courtyard, but no bar and no pool. All twenty rooms are air-conditioned and have cable TV. There is a hotel travel agent who can help book tours for you, but the hotel also has Internet, fax, and telephone services if you prefer to book things yourself. Singles are $51, doubles are $62, and triples are $73 (though rates may vary slightly by season). All rooms are clean, well kept, and comfortable. Laundry service is available. Plaza Loreto is a fine, relatively inexpensive hotel in a tremendously convenient central location. However, because the hotel is in the center of town, rooms facing the street may be a little noisy, especially at nighttime. This is a great value and a quality hub for adventure-seeking travelers.

*Location: Miguel Hidalgo*

*Phone: 613-135-0280; Fax: 613-135-0855*

*E-mail: hotelplazaloreto@prodigy.net.mx*

*Web: www.loreto.com/hotelplaza*

Photo by Doug Ogle

Iguana wall mural at the Iguana Inn

## Iguana Inn

The Iguana Inn is a set of four bungalows located one block from the water and two blocks from the central square. Every bungalow comes with air-conditioning, two beds, a basic kitchenette, and recently renovated tile bathrooms. The bungalows surround a spacious courtyard with a central fountain, and there are barbeque facilities available to all guests. The office advertises a complimentary video library and a book exchange with over 200 books. The clean, quiet, and comfortable bungalows cost approximately $50 per night for two people, and each extra guest is an extra $5 per night—a bargain compared to the competition. Proprietors **Mike and Julie Ramos** are amicable and accommodating, and Iguana will not disappoint.

*Location: Av. Benito Juárez and Calle Davis*

*Phone: 613-135-1627*

*E-mail: iguanainn@yahoo.com*

*Web: www.iguanainn.com*

## La Damiana Inn

La Damiana Inn is a bohemian traveler's dream: colorful, friendly, low-key, and artfully furnished. Once a large family residence (built in 1916), it was recently renovated by expat **Debora Simmons** and Baja native **Gerardo Lieras**. Damiana feels like a home—warm and inviting with a spacious common area, a shared open-air kitchen, a front and back patio, and a garden area. Massive rocking chairs (from the original family) and shelves of books are scattered throughout. Five individualized air-conditioned rooms offer a variety of sleeping accommodations and range from $52 to $60 per night—a great value. With its "old Mexico" stucco and décor, Damiana feels secluded from the inside, but the inn is centrally located on Francisco I. Madero just south of Avenida Miguel Hidalgo, a stone's throw from the plaza and the Malecón. Just look for La Damiana's bright yellow, hand-painted shingle. You might have to step past Isabelle, the mellow family dog, to get to your room, but it will be worth it for the simple luxuries awaiting: cotton bedding, thick towels, wireless access, really decent coffee, and a little taste of two eras well blended.

*Location: On Fco. I. Madero just south of Av. Miguel Hidalgo*
*Phone: 613-135-0356*
*E-mail: ladamianainn@yahoo.com*
*Web: www.ladamianainn.com*

## Desert Inn Loreto (formerly La Pinta Loreto)

Desert Inn Loreto is a pleasant, waterfront hotel located on the outskirts of town. It feels removed from the town center, and is almost an entirely self-contained world complete with a beautiful outdoor pool area,

Elegant Terns

restaurants, bar, and recreational activities that you can arrange through the hotel. The rooms, desperately needing updating, start at $90 for a hacienda single, or $113 for a single room in one of the villas. They are adequate but nothing exceptional, with air-conditioning and all expected amenities, though the "satellite cable TV" is actually just a few Spanish stations and one U.S. news channel. The hotel is somewhat run down compared to what you'd expect for the price. The beachfront location is its best feature. Full room service, maid service, and a travel desk that can help you arrange activities during your stay are all pluses. Every year, La Pinta hosts the **Vagabundos Dorado Fishing Tournament** in early July *(www.vagabundos.com)*, making it another favorite for fishermen.

*Location: Calle Davis*
*Phone: 800-800-9632 (From USA and Canada); 880-026-3605 (In Mexico)*
*Web: www.desertinns.com*

## Las Cabañas de Loreto

A half-block off the Malecón, Las Cabañas de Loreto is the perfect place for a small group to stay and enjoy the pleasant atmosphere of Loreto from the comfort of a personal cabaña. There are four cabañas costing $85 per night or $400 per week, each with two large comfy beds, and complete with a beautiful tiled bathroom and shower, TV, VCR, and a full kitchenette with a microwave, toaster, refrigerator, and coffee maker. If you really want to splurge, there is also the "Casa de Loreto"—with a minimum stay of one week at $2,000—that, with two master bedrooms (each with a bathroom) and a full-size kitchen, is perfect for two couples or a family of four. All guests of either the Casa or the cabañas are welcome to use the communal pool, hot tub, palapa, outdoor barbeque and tables, sink area, laundry area, and hammocks. Las Cabañas is an immaculate, sheltered property in a great location with a very self-contained, private feel—a fantastic alternative to a crowded resort. All of this, along with the extremely friendly and helpful owners, make Las Cabañas a splendid place to kick back and relax in Loreto.

*Location: One house off the Malecón on José M. Moreles*
*Phone: 613-135-1105*
*Web: www.lascabanasdeloreto.com*

## Olive Tree Villas

Olive Tree Villas is a set of condominiums located in Nopoló, several miles south of Loreto. Their clean facilities and the out-of-the-way location make Olive Tree an ideal location for a very quiet, simple vacation, and a great value. Three-bedroom condos are $145 per night, two-bedroom condos are $120 per night, and the one-bedroom condo is $65 per night. There is a pool and kitchen on the property, and every room comes air-conditioned with a TV and VCR.

*Location: Nopoló*

*Phone: 613-247-9105*

*Web: www.vacationrentals.com/vacation-rentals/10296.html*

## SuKasa Bungalows

**Joyce Clagett's** SuKasa Bungalows is anything but your average Loreto accommodation. SuKasa has two colorful private bungalows that rent for $65 per day, $440 per week. The bungalows are suitable for two to four people, with a king-size bed in the bedroom, a living room with couches that can be turned into two single beds, a fully stocked kitchen, and a patio. The only problem is that the bungalows do not have air-conditioning. Although every room has a ceiling fan, it could get very hot in the hottest months of the summer. There is also a two-story, two-bedroom, two-bathroom main house—far bigger and more comfortable for a larger group—that ranges from $770 to $910 per week, depending on the season. The complex is located on the Malecón, and is a terrific beachfront property that offers splendid views of the Sea of Cortés. There are nice palm trees and relaxing hammocks strewn about the property, and overall, SuKasa is a reasonably priced, nice place to enjoy your time in Loreto with a lover or with the family.

*Location: Blvd. López Mateos and*
*    Fernando Jordán*

*Phone: 613-135-0490*

*E-mail: sukasa@prodigy.net.mx or*
*    sukasa_bungalows@hotmail.com*

*Web: www.loreto.com/sukasa*

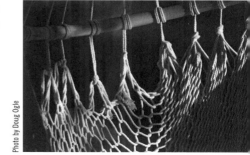

Photo by Doug Ogle

# HIGH-END

## Hotel Posada de las Flores

The premier hotel in Loreto (one of three locations in a chain), Posada de las Flores blends gracefully into the historic town center, combining traditional colonial Mexican architecture with all the modern luxuries of a five-star hotel. When you enter Posada de las Flores you feel like you are entering another world. The thick wooden beams combined with handmade tiles, elegant paintings, and ceramics make every corridor and room unique and beautiful. Rates change depending on the season, but standard rooms (small and dim, with antique furnishings) cost $150 to $180 per night, and Junior suites range from $230 to $260 per night. Each of the fifteen rooms has a satellite TV, telephone, coffee service, and a chic bathroom. There is a tapas bar on the ground level connected to the lobby, and on the rooftop there is a full bar and Italian restaurant called **Vecchia Roma**. Most notable is the glass-bottom pool directly above the lobby, from which you can gaze down into the town square and across to the mission. Posada de las Flores is much more suitable for a romantic getaway than a vacation with the kids.

*Location: Salvatierra and Fco. I. Madero, Col. Centro*

*Phone: 613-135-1162*

*Web: www.posadadelasflores.com*

The rooftop pool of Hotel Posada de las Flores provides a breathtaking view of the surrounding area.

Photo by Doug Ogle

Poolside at The Inn at Loreto Bay is a great place to unwind.

## The Inn at Loreto Bay

An iconic bell tower reminiscent of the one in the historic heart of Loreto identifies this top-notch **Nopoló** resort and is visible from a distance. Perfect for both adults and children, the inn offers a host of activities, including boating, water volleyball, beach volleyball, kayaking, snorkeling, scuba, swimming in two different pools, or relaxing under a palapa on the beach. Equipment for these activities can be borrowed, or rented for a nominal charge, from a small beachfront station. Each of the 155 rooms and suites offers a view of the Sea of Cortés and features Mexican furnishings alongside spacious, strikingly modern marble-and-glass bathrooms. Amenities include air-conditioning, ceiling fan, digital safe box, satellite TV, mini bar, and hair dryer. Three on-site restaurants—buffet, gourmet, and poolside restaurant/bar—are available to satiate any visitor's appetite. Rates range from $125 to $250 per night. The modest but sufficient fitness center is currently under renovation. On-site meeting facilities can accommodate functions for up to 300 people. The main restaurant, **Salvatierra**, serves excellent food in a beautiful beachfront location and the **Blue Whale Pool Bar** is also great for lunch and snacks. The Inn will be undergoing a major renovation that will only enhance this beautiful resort property.

*Location: Blvd. Misión de Loreto, Nopoló*

*Phone: 866-850-0333 for reservations (From USA or Canada); 800-507-5969 or 011-52-613-133-0010 (In Mexico)*

*Web: www.innatloretobay.com*

# BED AND BREAKFAST

## Loreto Playa Bed and Breakfast

Tucked away in quiet North Loreto on Davis Street after it turns into a dirt road, **Paulette and Robert Gochie's** B&B is a reigning favorite for visitors who know what's what. The facility includes two suites, each with king-size beds, satellite television/DVD, bathrooms with large tubs, and terraces overlooking the sea. The downstairs suite is the smaller of the two, but provides ample space and relaxation for a couple in search of a romantic retreat. The upper suite is a traveler's gem, an expanded version of the one below it, boasting a two-level terrace complete with dining and sunbathing amenities. Paulette is the homemaking mother you wish you had: she has decorated the space to be as comfortable, welcoming, and as down-home as you could imagine finding this far south on the Baja Peninsula. And her breakfast quesadillas simply can't be beat. For romantics or travelers in search of a quieter scene, Loreto Playa is as good as it gets. Guests and non-guests alike should not miss the weekly art classes held in the B&B's spacious and airy garage, often taught by guests artists from all over Mexico and across the globe. Suites run from $145 to $255 per night and are all non-smoking. Full breakfast is included in the rate.

*Location: North Loreto on Calle Davis*

*Phone: 613-135-1129*

*Web: www.loretoplaya.com*

# R.V. PARKS

## El Moro R.V. Park

El Moro offers spaces for anywhere from a day to a year. Prices may vary based on season and availability. If there's room at Rivera del Mar, try there first.

*Location: One block from the Malecón on Rosendo Robles No. 8*

*Phone/Fax: 613-135-0542*

*E-mail: fomixlor@lapaz.cromwell.com.mx*

*Web: www.loreto.com/elmoro*

## Rivera del Mar R.V. Park & Camping

Rivera del Mar is a 24-hour secured R.V. park a short distance from the beach, and the nicest of its kind in the Loreto vicinity. Their 25-space property is clean, comfortable and has all the necessary amenities: electricity, hot water, and sewage. Only some of the spaces are shaded, but there are outdoor lounge areas with a barbecue, which makes a perfect place to relax and stay cool. Full hookups cost $14 per day ($12 per day for a week's stay), while a spot with no hook-up is $12 per day ($10 per day for a week's stay). In the summer months, air-conditioning is available for an extra $3. Other features include water drainage ($5) and filling ($7 for 12–15 gallons), fax ($1 per sheet) and Internet access ($1.50 per hour). For campers, tent-only space is available for $5 per person. If you aren't staying in the R.V. park but are in need of a hot shower, Rivera del Mar will let you rinse for $4. Enjoy three meals a day at the **Café Sagitareo**, a local favorite and popular restaurant for campers and residents alike.

*Location: Five blocks north of the central plaza on Av. Fco. I. Madero*

*Phone: 613-135-0718*

*E-mail: lanyvall@yahoo.com.mx*

*Web: www.riveradelmar.com*

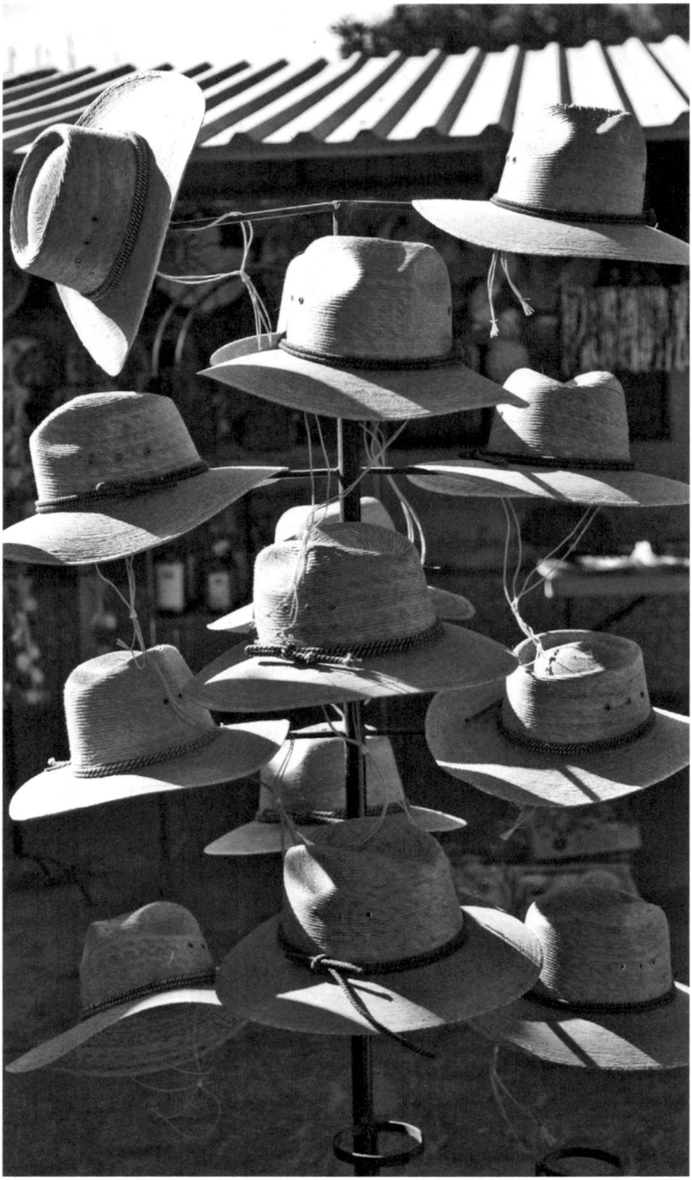

Photo by Doug Ogle

# 6

# Goods and Services

- Accessories/Miscellaneous
- Arts and Crafts
- Clothing
- Fishing Supplies
- Jewelry
- Secondhand Goods
- Souvenirs
- Sporting Goods

# ACCESSORIES/MISCELLANEOUS

## Claudia

Though you might be put off by the purple awning, Claudia is an interesting store to explore. Advertised as a store for *regalos* (gifts), it certainly lives up to the enigmatic title. Filled with dolls, mini-bikes, balls, children's beauty accessories, and toys galore, it is a wonderful place to take children in search of something fun to play with. It also doubles as a basic baby and toddler outfitter, complete with baby clothes, bottles, and stuffed animals. To top things off, it takes its gift store status seriously, and therefore has plenty of wrapping paper and gift-wrapping accessories. This is a multi-purpose store worth visiting if you have young children.

*Location: Av. Miguel Hidalgo No. 17, Col. Centro*
*Phone: 613-135-0252*

## Dulcería "SheKina"

This fascinating store is located several blocks past the main traffic light. It offers a wide array of items, but does not seem to specialize in any. The eclectic inventory includes aluminum foil, plastic cups, piñatas, water balloons, drinks, party supplies, and candy. If you have young children with you, and need an easy way to entertain them, stop by this place. It will certainly have something of interest. The attendants speak only Spanish, but the owner is a wonderful man who would be more than happy to assist in breaking the language barrier.

*Location: Av. Miguel Hidalgo, Col. Centro*

Photo by Doug Ogle

# ARTS & CRAFTS

## Conchita's Curios

Conchita's is an enormous arts-and-crafts store offering simple gifts, rustic furniture, home and office decorations, and much more. Original handmade pieces are shipped to Loreto from every part of Mexico. The shop is divided into many different rooms. Don't let the air-conditioned entry keep you from exploring everything Conchita's has to offer: furniture, ceramics, paintings, metal work, mirrors, lamps, and hundreds of other rare, random pieces made out of everything from shell to cactus. Some of the more impressive collections include black clay from Oaxaca, Talavera-style ceramic plates from Puebla, and remarkable replica cave paintings made by a local artist in Loreto. Even a wooden table made before the Mexican Revolution is for sale. Overall, the items in the store are less expensive than you'd expect. Get lost in Conchita's, just a few blocks south of Av. Miguel Hidalgo, the main drag. There's a lot to see here that you can't find anywhere else.

*Location: Misioneros and Fernando Jordán S/N, Col. Centro*
*Hours: 9:00 a.m.–1:00 p.m.; 4:00 p.m.–8:00 p.m.*
*Phone: 613-135-1054*

## El Alacrán

El Alacrán is technically two stores next door to one another—a private modern art gallery and an arts-and-crafts/souvenir store. The latter offers handmade crafts and silver jewelry as well as hand-designed cotton T-shirts, sweatshirts, and shorts. The gallery features the owners' own abstract expressionist paintings—vibrant, whimsical works which all art lovers should at least come in to take a look at, if not buy. Each painting sells for a few hundred dollars, with prices varying depending on the size of the piece.

*Location: On the cobblestone part of Salvatierra, next door to the mission*
*Hours: 9:30 a.m.–1:30 p.m., 2:30 p.m.–7:00 p.m. (Mon.–Sat.)*
*Phone: 613-135-0029*

## Galería Loreto

Canadian painters **Tom and Donna Dickson** have been wintering in Loreto for the better part of ten years and have recently moved to the peninsula year round. Galería Loreto is the result of the time they've spent in the area and their passion for the beauty of Mexican life. Tom is an experienced oil painter whose works have been displayed in renowned galleries in British Columbia. His works of Mexican subjects deserve equal acclaim. His perfect eye for light brings to life his recent series of Loretan scenes, most notably of the town's iconic clock tower. Donna's watercolor works depict equally wonderful local scenes and have similarly graced the walls of multiple Canadian galleries. True art lovers and prospective homeowners alike owe this gallery a visit. It is a modest venue which allows the artists' work to speak entirely for itself.

*Location: On the corner of Benito Juárez and Pino Suárez*

*Hours: October–June, 9:30 a.m.–1:00 p.m., and 3:30 p.m.–5:30 p.m. (Tue.–Sat.)*

*Phone: 613-135-1064*

*Web: www.dicksonsgallery.com*

## La Iguana—ARTE

La Iguana offers miscellaneous arts-and-crafts pieces such as decorated, handmade items; table centerpieces; wall adornments; and much more. Upstairs is a large selection of Loreto and Baja T-shirts and tank tops. You're bound to walk by while in town, so definitely stop in, especially if you have a knack for getting your hands on rare finds.

*Location: Corner of Av. Miguel Hidalgo and Fco. I. Madero*

*Hours: 9:00 a.m.–8:00 p.m.*

*Phone: 613-135-1355*

*E-mail: adriannaloreto@yahoo.com.mx*

## Vesubio

This local arts-and-crafts store is definitely worth checking out. Vesubio offers a wide range of expertly handcrafted work, specializing in goods from Guadalajara. Everything in the store is beautiful, whether it is rustic furniture, Mexican artwork, wooden picture frames, light fixtures, or candle holders. The prices are reasonable, and it is certainly not a place where you will get the average tourist item, as the store is frequented by locals. As long as your Spanish is up to par, then head into Vesubio and feast your eyes upon some truly beautiful authentic Mexican arts and crafts.

*Location: Fco. I. Madero No. 56, Col. Centro*

*Phone: 613-135-1132*

# CLOTHING

## Fashion's

One of the nicer clothing stores in town, Fashion's has men's and women's apparel and American brands at American prices. Denim and swimwear are staples here, along with button-down shirts and even a small selection of formal attire. Do not come here if you are looking for a bargain. Do come here if you are in need of good-looking threads that you might otherwise find in a department store. Footwear and other accessories are available, too.

*Location: On Salvatierra, one-half block before the main traffic light coming into town*

*Hours: 9:30 a.m.–1:30 p.m., 4:00 p.m.– 8:30 p.m. (Mon.–Fri.); 9:30 a.m.– 8:30 p.m. (Sat.)*

*Phone: 613-135-2047*

## Paileva

Air-conditioned and filled with high-quality clothes, Paileva is a basic clothing store that closely resembles one you would find in a mall in the United States. Stocked with pants, including khakis and slacks, summer dresses, shirts, and button-ups, Paileva has plenty of good clothes to buy. A small, simple store good for purchasing basic clothes similar to those you would find in the United States.

*Location: Benito Juárez S/N, Col. Centro*

Photo by Doug Ogle

Art influences art: a Frida Kahlo-inspired dress.

## Tayli's

A modest seafoam-green storefront on Salvatierra, Tayli's offers arguably the best selection of intimate apparel and lingerie to ladies in the area. A small but impressive selection of bras, panties, and lingerie sets can be found inside for $20 to $30. Though it seems to serve a primarily local clientele, ladies in search of new undergarments will be satisfied with what they find here.

*Location: On Salvatierra just before the main traffic light coming into town*

# FISHING SUPPLIES

## Ferre-Mar Loreto

This shop is the place to go if you are a fisherman looking for rods, reels, lures, hooks, lines, or sinkers. Other than mechanics, this is "Equipment Central" for all things fishing. The colorful blue-green shop covered in signs is hard to miss.

*Location: On the western end of Benito Juárez coming into town*
*Open: 8:00 a.m.–1:30 p.m., 3:00 p.m.–7:00 p.m. (Mon–Sat.)*

# JEWELRY

## Gecko's

Kathleen Hill runs several businesses from this Miguel Hidalgo location and Gecko's has many interesting items including her locally crafted jewelry made from semi-precious stones, pearls, and crystals.

*Location: On Miguel Hidalgo across from McLulu's*
*Phone: 613-135-2505*

## Juda

This tiny shop just around the corner from La Cascada and across the street from Pachamama's designs custom-made jewelry using amber, topaz, and opals. They are able to do work with precious stones as well from their store in Cabo San Lucas. They offer a free Mexican Fire Opal charm to all customers.

*Location: Emiliano Zapata just north of Salvatierra*
*Phone: 613-116-4149*

## Silver Desert (Desierto de Plata)

This jewelry store is true to its name: what you will find here is silver jewelry galore. But Silver Desert goes beyond the typical expectations for a Mexican jewelry store, with higher-quality wares in more-original designs. The primarily handmade goods originate not only from Mexico but also more distant parts of the Latin world, including a brightly colored line of fig-seed jewelry from a Colombian designer. Semiprecious stones, pearls, and shells are other common additions to the silver jewelry found here. Visitors looking for stylish Mexican jewelry are likely to find something here worthy of any fine jewelry collection. Visa and Mastercard accepted.

*Location: Salvatierra No. 36 next to the bank*
*Hours: 9:00 a.m.–2:00 p.m. and 3:00 p.m.–8:30 p.m.*
*Phone: 613-135-0684*

## Taxco

Taxco has a great selection of silver jewelry of all kinds in its small shop on Salvatierra.

*Location: Salvatierra No. 59*
*Phone: 613-135-1082*

## Tony's Silver

Tony's Silver is one of the biggest stores on Salvatierra and perhaps in all of Loreto. It has a very large selection of silver jewelry and well-known Talavera ceramic items from Guadalajara.

*Location: Corner of Salvatierra and Colegio*
*Phone: 613-135-1400*
*Hours: 9:00 a.m.–8:30 p.m.*

Photos by Doug Ogle

Besides jewelry, Tony's Silver has a huge selection of crafts to choose from.

# SECONDHAND GOODS

### Segunda Alexandra

This indoor-outdoor makeshift secondhand pawnshop may look like a scrap yard at first glance, but it has a wide variety of useful and inexpensive items. Their inventory changes slightly from day to day, but they always have a good supply of TVs, kitchen appliances, furniture, and bikes. The main attraction is their huge stockpile of shoes and clothes. If you look long enough you are certain to find something worth buying, and you will get it for a bargain. A great place to go if you need to re-outfit yourself but do not want to spend much money.

*Location: Av. Miguel Hidalgo at Independencia*

## SOUVENIRS

### Avenida Salvatierra

Named after the founder of Loreto, *Avenida Salvatierra* is the main street into town. At the traffic light (at Independencia), it suddenly becomes a cobblestone pedestrian-only street. Drivers usually continue seamlessly to the right onto Avenida Miguel Hidalgo, never noticing they've left Salvatierra.

However, once on foot, visitors should certainly check out the true Salvatierra. Rows of neatly trimmed trees create a continuous arch that shades your way down the old road as you come upon shop after shop of souvenirs—

A weaver spins wool for rugs and blankets at The Blanket Factory located at Salvatierra and Colegio.
Photo by Doug Ogle

truly "Tourist Central." Most are open every day from 10:00 a.m. to 8:00 p.m., with shorter hours on Sundays. Don't take the posted hours too literally, as many shop owners like to open and close on their own schedules.

Vendors sell sombreros, shot glasses, leather goods, ponchos, straw hats, jewelry, chessboards, plates, decorative boxes, T-shirts. and even specialty vanilla extracts from Veracruz. You get the idea. There are a great number of stores from which to buy these common arts and crafts and some of the blankets are woven locally by the vendors. More shops appear to be coming soon with a new series of storefronts being built on a small side street just off of Salvatierra where it first becomes a pedestrian "mall."

Continuing down the street will bring you to the historic section of Loreto, complete with the Mission and some original buildings. The original Salvatierra is certainly worth checking out; just decide whether you want a sombrero before you go, because temptation can often get the better of you.

## SPORTING GOODS

### Deportes Blazer

Kitty-corner from Mike's Bar and a block away from the Malecón, Deportes Blazer is the best Loreto has to offer in the sporting goods department. Blazer is not specialized, but rather has a diverse selection of soccer, snorkel, and camping equipment, and quite a bit of fishing gear. When the manager noticed a shortage of music stores in Loreto he decided to hang some guitars in his store, too. You won't find hiking boots, jackets, or any fancy outdoor apparel here. Clothing and apparel is relatively limited, but Deportes Blazer is the place to look if you are in need of miscellaneous outdoor accessories.

*Location: Av. Miguel Hidalgo No. 23*
*Hours: 9:00 a.m.–8:00 p.m. (Mon.–Sat.)*
*Phone: 613-135-0911; 613-100-3598 (Cell)*

A string of garlic and chili peppers

# 7

# Practical Goods and Services

- Banking
- Beauty Salons
- Books/DVDs
- Business Consulting
- Courier Service
- Emergency and Medical Contacts
- Groceries
- Home/Office
- Internet Cafés
- Pharmacies
- Photography
- Plumber/Electrician/Hardware
- Post Office
- Public Library
- Telephones
- Veterinarians

# BANKING

## BBVA Bancomer

This has the only ATM machine currently in town, although another branch of this bank will be opening soon. Most cards accepted. It is located in a small room to the right of the main entrance. Lines at the bank can be long and we advise getting cash through the ATM whenever possible.

*Location: Corner of Fco. I. Madero and Salvatierra*

*Hours: 8:30 a.m.–4:00 p.m. (Mon.–Fri.); exchange hours 8:30 a.m.–2:30 p.m.*

*Phone: 613-135-0014 and 613-135-0015*

## Banamex

Not open as of this printing, but soon to be opened on Salvatierra, next to the main PEMEX.

# BEAUTY SALONS

## Norma's Salon & Spa

Offering haircuts, color, manicures, pedicures, massages, and beauty and bath products, Norma's is the place to go for looking your best. It is known to be the social hub of Loreto. The services are excellent and the prices are reasonable. Credit cards accepted.

*Location: Av. Miguel Hidalgo between Fco. I. Madero and Misionero*

*Hours: 9:00 a.m.–6:00 p.m. (Mon.–Sat.)*

*E-mail: normas_salon@msn.com*

# BOOKS/DVDS

## Baja Books

No, there isn't a Barnes & Noble in Loreto, yet. But for a store made from one man's private collection—and the only bookstore in Loreto—you should have no problem finding a reliable beach companion at Baja Books. Old paperbacks are stacked on every shelf, table, windowsill, chair, or countertop, and in the back room you can find almost every Baja- or Loreto-specific guidebook, pamphlet, novel, map, or periodical. Definitely ask for help if you are looking for a specific book—or if you're looking for any book, for that matter. You'll certainly find it quicker, and you might discover a few unexpected literary surprises.

*Location: At the intersection of Av. Miguel Hidalgo and Fco. I. Madero, just around the corner from Café Ole*

*Hours: 8:00 a.m.–7:00 p.m.*

*Phone: 613-105-9285*

### DVD Máximo

Though there are several video stores in Loreto, DVD Máximo not only has the widest selection of movies and new releases, it also is the only one that has everything in DVD rather than VHS. DVDs are on sale for $10 each or $30 for four. A two-day rental is $2.50, with a late fee of $1.50 per day. And don't forget 2 for 1 Tuesdays. DVD Máximo is the place to go for movies, and has all of your Hollywood favorites with English subtitles.

*Location: On Benito Juárez and Marqués de León*

*Hours: 3:00 p.m.–10:00 p.m.(Mon.–Fri.); 10:00 a.m.–10:00 p.m. (Sat.–Sun.)*

## BUSINESS CONSULTING

### BajaBOSS, Business One Stop Solutions

**Nellie Hutchinson**, a local dynamo, owns BajaBOSS, a business services company for anyone living, working, or doing business in Loreto. Nellie can provide information and aid for anything legal or financial you need assistance with, including starting a business, setting up accounts, immigration, visas, and investments—in English or Spanish. Anything you need to know about accelerating and facilitating your life and business in Mexico, she and her staff can help you. Nellie's headquarters on the Malecón are also home to **Dorado Properties**, which handles property purchases and sales all across the southern Baja Peninsula. Finally, Nellie runs a small, six-room hotel ($60/night), furnished in traditional rustic Mexican style, with comfortable king-size beds, and a rooftop tapas and sushi bar to boot.

*Location: Blvd. López Mateos between Jordán and Paseo Hidalgo*

*Hours: 9:00 a.m.–7:00 p.m. (Mon.–Fri.)*

*Phone: 613-135-0309 (Mexico); 602-628-2920 (U.S. Cell)*

*E-mail: info@bajaboss.com*

*Web: www.bajaboss.com*

# COURIER SERVICE

## Estafeta Local Courier Service

Deliveries go out in the afternoon. Typical delivery time is one to three days to the peninsula, and three to seven days to the Mexican mainland, USA and Canada.

*Location: Misioneros*

*Hours: 9:00 a.m.–4:00 p.m. (Mon.–Fri.)*

*Phone: 613-135-0904*

# EMERGENCY AND MEDICAL CONTACTS

### Centro de Salud

State-run 24-hour hospital; cost per visit approximately $50; emergency services and non-emergency appointments. Cash only for all services; all currencies accepted.

*Location: Calle Salvatierra in front of the gas station*

*Phone: 613-135-0039*

*E-mail: algreen42@hotmail.com*

### Federal Police

*Location: Nopoló*

*Phone: 613-133-0794*

*Hours: 9:00 a.m.–3:00 p.m. (Mon.–Fri.)*

### Municipal Police

*Location: Paseo Tamaral, next to University of La Paz Loreto Campus*

*Phone: 613-135-0035*

### Paramedics/Ambulance/Fire

*Location: Paseo Tamaral, next door to the Police Station*

*Phone: 613-135-1566*

## Doctors On Call 24 Hours

Doctors speak limited English. $40 per visit. Cash only.

### Dr. Estanislao Collins

*Phone: 613-135-1293 (Main); 044-613-104-3600 (Cell)*

**Dr. Oscar Green**

*Phone: 613-135-0477 (Main); 044-613-104-3562 (Cell)*

**Dr. Primo Maraver**

*Phone: 044-613-104-0810 (Cell)*

**Dr. Fernando Lopez Pineda Orozco**

*Phone: 613-135-1498 (Main); 044-613-109-0165 (Cell)*
*E-mail: fdolopezpineda@prodigy.net.mx*

## Concerned About Medical Care?

The author awoke one fine, clear, hot Sunday morning with an eye infection that was obviously in need of immediate medical attention. We went to the farmacia to get something for it but its condition was such that even the pharmacy required that a doctor be seen. About to catch a plane in a couple of hours, this was not a welcomed prospect. After all, in the United States, even the smallest visit to a clinic would entail long waits, insurance, medical histories, and considerable expense. I could only imagine the hassle of getting this looked at in Loreto.

We walked into the seemingly empty Centro de Salud hospital and clinic across from the PEMEX coming into town and asked to see the doctor. In literally less than two minutes Dr. Fernando Lopez Pineda Orozco came out to greet us and in excellent English asked me about my problem. After several probing questions and a five-minute exam of my person and my eye he prescribed an antibiotic ointment and drops to ease my obvious discomfort. Cost of my visit? $30. I was back at the pharmacy twenty minutes after I left, got the medication I needed, and two days later my eye was well again.

This experience left an indelible impression on us. Ironically, considering my fear of inferior health care and facilities in these parts, I was professionally treated in a way I could only wish would occur in the United States, with service that was fast, efficient, and affordable.

To give Loreto the type of facilities it really needs as a growing resort town, a new hospital is being completed right off the highway as you enter Loreto from the south, where you curve into Avenida Salvatierra. The new $8 million dollar facility will eventually have 36 beds and will provide internal medicine, general medicine, surgical care, and high-risk deliveries with one labor and delivery suite, one operating room, one surgeon, one obstetrician, and one pediatrician. There will also be x-ray and lab facilities.

### Dentists

**Dr. Eduardo Velázquez Anzaldúa (known as Dr. Lalo)**

Dr. Velázquez Anzaldúa speaks limited English and treats most of the North American patients. His work is reportedly excellent and extremely reasonable in cost.

*Location: Fco. I. Madero No. 64*

*Phone: 613-135-0115*

*Hours: 9:00 a.m.–1:00 p.m.; 4:00 p.m.–6:30 p.m. (Mon.–Sat.)*

### Red Cross (Cruz Roja Mexicana)

La Cruz Roja provides ambulances and emergency and disaster relief services.

*Phone: 613-135-1111*

# GROCERIES

### Dali

Dali is a specialty food store/service that originally was a restaurant supplier and now caters to local residents. With an impressive list of hundreds of different items, you can order just about anything your stomach desires.

*Location: On Fco. I Madera just north of Av. Miguel Hidalgo*

*Hours: 8:00 a.m.–5:00 p.m. (Mon.–Fri.); 8:00 a.m.–1:00 p.m. (Sat.)*

*E-mail: daliloreto@prodigy.net.mx (menu available)*

### El Pescador

El Pescador is the best supermarket you'll find in Loreto. Meats, produce, cosmetics, liquor, refreshments, canned foods—anything a supermarket should have, you can find here, however, maybe not in the quantity or quality of an American-style supermarket. This is also the best place in town to get ice. There is a small pharmacy and tobacco counter together (say what?) in the front. El Pescador has insufficient parking and many believe the location of this grocery will change in coming years. Technically, there is another market simply called Pescador that you might see first on your way into town, only a few blocks west from the main grocery. Generally, when people refer to the "Pescador," they are talking about the bigger one.

*Location: At the traffic light where Salvatierra turns into Av. Miguel Hidalgo*
*Hours: 7:30 a.m.–10:30 p.m.*
*Phone: 613-135-0060*

## El Portón

This very nice small market and convenience store is the only store currently in **Nopoló**. It is poised to stock more and different items as The Villages of Loreto Bay proceeds with development. Nevertheless it carries just about anything you might need in a pinch.

*Location: Misión de San Ignacio, Nopoló*

## Farmer's Market

The Farmer's Market used to be located on Highway 1 north of town but has recently been relocated to the Río Loreto in the **Zaragoza** neighborhood. Take a right on Francisco I. Madero until the road dips into and across the arroyo. You will see the market stalls to the right on the bank of the arroyo. On Saturdays, the locals gather together to sell produce, as well as some clothing and electronics. This farmer's market started out as a few locals selling their goods, and over time grew dramatically. This is an opportunity to witness the hustle and bustle of the Loretanos in action.

*Location: Zaragoza neighborhood on Fco. I. Madero*
*Hours: Only on Saturday morning*

## Qué Buena Frutería

The produce headquarters, Qué Buena is the best place in town for fresh fruit and vegetables. Perfect for an apple on the go or for preparing a home-cooked meal, this frutería also has a wall of spices and shelves full of nonperishables. Some practical kitchen cleaning supplies and plastic cups are also available, and a small meat and cheese counter makes this a well-rounded, much-needed place for a pit stop.

*Location: Just before Fco. I. Madero on Benito Juárez*
*Phone: 613-135-1166*

## Tienda Isste

This government-subsidized grocery store has all the basics—cosmetics, cleaning products, and canned foods, but the selection is usually sparse and picked over and El Pescador may be a better choice for finding what you are looking for. The one advantage it has is its location near the plaza.

*Location: Just up Fco. I. Madero from the Municipal building in the main square*
*Hours: 8:00 a.m.–8:00 p.m. (Mon.–Sat.); 8:00 a.m.–2:00 p.m. (Sun.)*

# HOME/OFFICE

## La Papelería

La Papelería is located just on the edge of town as you approach on the main street. It is a great place to purchase any basic office supplies while staying in the Loreto area. It is inexpensive and well stocked, with pleasant employees. Make sure you have basic Spanish-speaking skills before you enter; it can be hard to mime a clipboard.

*Location: Salvatierra and Ayuntamiento*
*Hours: 9:30 a.m.–8:00 p.m. (Mon.–Sat.)*
*Phone: 613-135-0221, 613-135-0658*

## Papelería y Copias Californias

While the store appears from the outside sign to specialize in copies, which it does in both black-and-white and color, it actually has an amazing collection of school and art supplies as well. If you are looking to outfit a student or gather basic office supplies, this is the place to go. They have everything from backpacks, folders, and notepads to compasses and calculators. In the art supplies department, they have pens and crayons of every color, heaps of construction and tissue paper, and basic tools such as glue and scissors.

*Location: On Salvatierra between Independencia and Ayuntamiento, Col. Centro*
*Phone: 613-135-0221*

## Tienda Electrónica

Though the store lacks a back warehouse and is mostly filled with boxes, it actually has a good selection of electronics, if you can successfully navigate through the maze. The store sells cell phones, car stereos, TVs, printers, digital cameras, speakers, kitchen appliances, computer accessories, DVD players, irons, and air-conditioners. One of the most comprehensive electronics stores in Loreto, it is our recommendation if you are in need of any of the items mentioned above.

*Location: On Independencia, north of Av. Miguel Hidalgo*

## Yamuni

Yamuni is a chain throughout Baja with two locations in Loreto. Yamuni carries electronics, modern furniture, and kitchen furnishings such as counters and cabinets. A modern, air-conditioned store, it is a good place to check out if you are moving to Loreto and want to furnish your home.

*Location: Fco. I. Madero #16, corner of Benito Juárez and Magdalena de Kino, Col. Centro*

*Phone: 613-135-2120*

# INTERNET CAFÉS

## .COM

This air-conditioned Internet café has five computers with high-speed Internet access, a fax machine, a scanner, and a printer. However, the equipment is not of the highest quality, and they charge $2 per hour, twice as much as Ricardo's.

*Location: Next to Café Olé*

*Hours: 9:00 a.m.–9:00 p.m.*

## Café Internet

Café Internet has eight computers, a printer, scan/fax machine, telephone, and air-conditioning. The rate for Internet service is $2 per hour.

*Location: On Salvatierra, just past the PEMEX gas station on the left when entering town*

## Caseta Soledad Internet Café

Nine computers, two with full software, two printers, scan and fax service, long distance, and call service. Approximately $3 per hour.

*Location: Salvatierra just up the street from El Pescador*

*Hours: 9:00 a.m.–8:00 p.m. seven days a week*

*Phone: 613-135-0351*

*Fax: 613-135-0284*

### Ricardo's

Ricardo's has four computers with high-speed Internet access as well as a quality fax machine, scanner, and printer. It has plenty of fans to cool you down, but no air-conditioning. At $1 per hour it is the cheapest Internet we could find.

*Location: On the corner of Benito Juárez and Fco. I. Madero*
*Hours: 9:30 a.m.–8:30 p.m.*

# PHARMACIES

There are four farmacias in Loreto, three on Salvatierra as you come into town and one located in the Miramar section of Loreto just off of Highway 1 as you head north out of town.

### Farmacia de Las Californias

This shop is a more traditional drugstore with a limited pharmacy.

*Location: Salvatierra just west of El Pescador*
*Hours: 8:00 a.m.–10:00 p.m. (Daily)*
*Phone: 613-135-0341*

### Farmacia del Rosario

This is a full-fledged drugstore and pharmacy.

*Location: Two branches: One on Salvatierra almost directly across from*
   *El Pescador; the other on Benito Juárez at Misioneros*
*Hours: 8:00 a.m.–10:00 p.m. (Daily)*
*Phone: 613-135-0917*

### Farmacia Flores

This is a small limited inventory drugstore and pharmacy located a few blocks up Salvatierra towards Highway 1.

*Phone: 613-135-1321*

### Farmacia Similares

This is a pharmacy with a medical clinic attached, not really a drugstore.

*Location: Salvatierra at Marqués de León*
*Hours: Pharmacy: 8:30 a.m.–9:00 p.m. (Mon.–Sat.), 9:00 a.m.–3:00 p.m. (Sun.);*
   *Clinic: 9:00 a.m.–1:00 p.m. (Daily)*

*Phone: 613-135-1194*

# PHOTOGRAPHY

## Foto Video Professional

This is a camera shop and photo studio that is knowledgeable about the requirements of passport and visa photo requirements. This is not an instant photo shop and their photo service may take a day or two to get developed. Some Spanish helpful; cash only.

*Location: On Salvatierra at Ignacio Allende*

*Phone: 613-135-1725*

# PLUMBER/ELECTRICIAN/HARDWARE

## Ferretería Ayón Ruan y Asociados

Just before you get to the gas station when heading toward the water on *Salvatierra* is Ayón Ruan Ferretería, packed with metal, painting, plumbing, electric, and construction supplies. It's a small hardware store but it's got *tons* of stuff, and if you can communicate with the helpful staff, you should find exactly what you are looking for—whether it's an obscure type of screwdriver, nuts and bolts, a car jack, or any other hardware solution to your repair problems.

*Location: On Salvatierra on the way into town, before the PEMEX gas station*

*Hours: 8:00 a.m.–1:00 p.m., 3:00 p.m.–7:00 p.m.*

## Plomería y Electricidad

Located a few blocks past the main traffic light on your way out of town, this is a great place if you are in need of its plumbing and electrical services. The store offers a wide range of hardware: light bulbs, tools, saws, brooms, car maintenance supplies, etc. Do not expect to be graciously guided through the store by employees anxious to address your every need. This is a store that primarily services the locals. It is certainly not hostile to gringos, but only go if you know exactly what you need ahead of time. Otherwise it could make for some frustrating miscommunications.

*Location: Av. Miguel Hidalgo S/N between Calle Colegio and Independencia,*
*Col. Centro*

*Phone: 613-135-0762*

## POST OFFICE

Post office boxes available for rent.

*Location: Deportiva No. 13 between Salvatierra and Benito Juárez*

*Hours: 8:00 a.m.–3:00 p.m. (Mon.–Fri.)*

*Phone: 613-135-0647*

## PUBLIC LIBRARY

You can obtain a library card with proof of address. You'll need two passport-size pictures to create your ID card. Partial English spoken.

*Location: Fco. I. Madero, door on the corner of Fco. I. Madero and Plaza Juárez*

*Hours: 8:00 a.m.–3:00 p.m. (Mon.–Fri.)*

## TELEPHONES

Local pay phones bear the logo TELMEX. Phone cards are available at most stores in denominations of 50, 100, and 200 pesos. For national calls, it's $2.50 per minute; for international calls, $5 per minute. Collect calls from a pay phone will usually add a service charge of 30%.

## VETERINARIANS

### Veterinaria Loreto

This is the local vet (Dr. Juan Cortéz), the place for ranchers needing supplies for their livestock, and a traditional pet store.

*Location: On Salvatierra across from Hacienda Suites Hotel*

*Phone: 613-135-0912*

 **Bringing Pets to Loreto**

**Bringing your pet into Mexico is a fairly simple process. If you are flying in with your pet, all that is needed at customs is a Certificate of Health for your animal. If you are driving, you will also need to show papers that your pet is free of rabies in case you are asked.**

**How to Make a Call in Loreto**

With the advent of cell phones, making a simple telephone call has turned into a complicated assortment of possibilities. Questions to be answered include: where is the call originating from and being directed to, are you using a landline or a cell phone, and is the call local or long distance. If you want your cell phone to work in Mexico you need to arrange additional service (about $5 per month) with your cell phone provider. This only allows your phone to operate in Mexico; there are usually roaming charges involved for cellular service. You can also buy a cheap disposable cell phone in Mexico and purchase a chip with minutes.

Here is our quick guide to making calls to and from Loreto.

### United States to Mexico

*To a Landline:* 011 + 52 + Area Code + Number

*To a Cell Phone:* 011 + 52 + 1 + Area Code + Number (The extra "1" after the Mexico country code 52 is critical if calling into Mexico to a cell phone.)

### Mexico to United States

001 + Area Code + Number

### Within Mexico

*Landline to Landline:*

**Local Calls:** Area Code + Number
**Long Distance Calls:** 01 + Area Code + Number

*Landline to Cell Phone:*

**Local Calls:** 044 + Area Code + Number
**Long Distance Calls:** 045 + Area Code + Number

*Cell Phone to Landline:*

**Local Calls:** This depends on the phone (really). Try the ten digit number first and if it doesn't work, try the seven digit number.
**Long Distance in Mexico:** 01 + Area Code + Number

*Cell Phone to Cell Phone:*

**Local Calls:** Area Code + Number
**Long Distance Calls:** Area Code + Number

Toll-free numbers do not work within Mexico. In order to call a toll-free number while in Mexico, substitute these codes (some charges may apply). For 800, dial 880; for 888, dial 881; for 877, dial 882; and for 866, dial 883.

**7**

**PRACTICAL GOODS AND SERVICES**

A sleepy sea lion on Coronado Island

# 8

# Islands

Loreto Bay's marine park, **Parque Nacional Marino Bahía de Loreto**, encompasses five *islas* (islands): **Coronado**, **Del Carmen**, **Danzante**, **Santa Catalina**, and **Monserrat**. Because this part of the Sea of Cortés has some of the most diverse marine life in the world and a local population that depends on the bay on many levels, commercial uses and environmental imperatives are often at odds. The park was created in an effort to strike a balance between competing interests, respecting the needs of the local communities while protecting natural resources.

The islands and surrounding waters are home to many species—some federally protected—including reptiles, land mammals, land and migratory birds (many under the protection of the **Sea of Cortés Islands Migratory Bird and Wildlife Refuge**), and "sport fish" such as marlin and swordfish. Loreto Bay also boasts Mexico's largest concentration of marine mammals—whales, sea lions, dolphins, turtles, and more. Camping is allowed on most of the islands except Isla del Carmen, which is privately owned.

## Isla Coronado

Whether you spend your time marveling at the spectacular coastal rock formations, getting up close to the sea lions, or relaxing on the crystal clear turquoise water and white sand beach, Isla Coronado will be well worth the boat ride out. There is one beach and, while it is certainly picturesque, it can be slightly uncomfortable to spend too much time there in the dog days of summer with no shade. There is decent snorkeling just a short swim offshore. On the north side of the beach is a hike that takes you to the peak of the central hill. Come to Coronado with a case of cerveza and treat yourself to a day of relaxation.

*Facts:* Coronado ("crowned island") is a small, arid island. It is 1.5 miles from Loreto, and is the most accessible of the park islands. There is a breed of lizard that is endemic to Coronado. The island, which used to be underwater, is scattered with fossils and coral remains.

*Advice:* Make sure you ask your guide to take you to the sea lion colony. Wear good footwear if you plan to go on the hike; the terrain changes from flat land to loose rocks to sand. If you are snorkeling, be sure to bring a snorkel mask if your tour does not include one.

*How to get there:* Almost every tour outfitter in town will offer some sort of excursion to Isla Coronado, and they are all essentially the same. If snorkeling is a priority, our favorite is **Dolphin Dive**, but be prepared

for steeper prices. If you just want cheap transportation to and from the island, you can show up at the marina in the morning where you'll find someone willing to take you. Keep in mind, however, that they most likely will not have permits, insurance, or safety gear.

## Isla del Carmen

Isla del Carmen is the biggest island in Baja California Sur. On a boat tour around Carmen, the topography changes from white-sand beaches to towering volcanic rock formations to cactus-laden, earth-toned, desert terrain. When the tide is low, small sea caves are visible on the east (back) side of the island. You can enter them in a panga, to view layers of sediment along the exposed cave walls, and shells fossilized in the rock overhead. In the channel of water between Carmen and Danzante, you may spot a pod of dolphins or some blue or fin whales. If not, the flying fish skipping on the surface next to your kayak will entertain. The rock formations at the two north points, **Punta Perico** and **Punta Lobos**, will surely impress. Finally, the adventurous can make camp on the northern face of the island at **Puerto de la Lancha** and hike up and along the jagged peaks.

Despite all of these natural wonders, Carmen is most famous for its abandoned salt mine at **Bahía Salinas**, which has been producing salt for centuries. It was occupied most recently by a company called **Salinas del Pacífico** until it shut down completely in 1983. Now the establishment, where miners once worked and lived, is a ghost town with demolished adobe, shattered glass, rusty machinery, and dusty relics from a widely unknown and relatively undocumented time and place in history. The original tracks and carts that brought the salt from the inland mine to the shore still exist, although the dock has rotted away. A shipwreck in the bay makes for exciting snorkeling when the tide isn't too high.

In the mid 1990s, the National Institute of Ecology and the Mexican Federal government agreed to make Isla del Carmen home to an endangered species of bighorn sheep. They were brought to this protected area for breeding; after their populations increase significantly, they will be reintroduced to the mainland. Consider yourself lucky if you manage to spot one—it's no easy feat.

*Facts:* One man actually owns the title on the entire island. He currently resides in Mexico City.

*Advice:* Since the island is technically private property, check with your panga driver or tour guide to make sure they won't get in trouble when you go exploring. At the very least, if you arrive at Bahía Salinas, ask the first person you see for permission to walk around.

*How to get there:* Getting a panga to take you to Isla del Carmen will not be cheap (over $100), but if you aren't sailing or kayaking, you have no other choice. Your best bet is to hire a panga at the marina. You can negotiate the price.

## Isla Danzante

Isla Danzante is the smallest island in Loreto's marine park, but is arguably the most beautiful. Danzante is known for its underwater terrain, featuring deep coral-coated walls, making it a perfect place for scuba diving and snorkeling. The adventurous can also hike to the top of the island, where pristine **Bahía Honda** is visible to the east, or explore the stunning geologic formation, **"La Puerta"** (The Door). Flora and fauna fanatics will enjoy the diverse vegetation, consisting of mangroves, elephant trees, prickly pear cactus, and much more. But on a day trip to Danzante, your best bet is to relax on the white-sand beaches. Honeymoon Cove is a gorgeous spot to anchor your sailboat, go for a swim, and bask in the sun.

*Facts:* Danzante is only 5 miles (8 km) southeast of **Puerto Escondido**, a 15-minute drive on Highway 1 from downtown Loreto.

*Advice:* The waters around Isla Danzante are some of the best for finding blue whales.

*How to get there:* Stop at Danzante on your kayaking excursion or plan a sailing trip for the day with **Baja Sail** departing from Puerto Escondido. If you want to wing it, drive to **Juncalito Beach** and ask around for a panga for hire.

## Isla Monserrat

Isla Monserrat gets its name from the serrated mountains on the island. Because it is quite far from Loreto, it is not recommended for a tourist who has only a week to explore the town but rather for adventurous sailors plying the Sea of Cortés. They tell us Monserrat has a reputation for quality lobster-hunting opportunities at nighttime. Also, **Yellowstone Beach**, which sits underneath vivid yellow sandstone and volcanic rock formations, is a prime anchorage for seafarers. **Las Galletas**, a pair of nearby islets, is a great snorkeling destination, where tropical fish, eels, and urchins are abundant. And as always, stellar sunset views will set the sky ablaze over the mainland mountaintops.

## Isla Santa Catalina

If you're someone interested in making the trip to Santa Catalina, the farthest island from Loreto, then there is nothing we can tell you about it that you probably don't already know. The hardcore naturalists and scientists have probably done their homework on the island's endemic species of "rattle-less" rattlesnake (whose rattle is degenerate, and therefore is shed naturally), as well as on the extremely large barrel cactus, cardón cactus forest, and rare iguana species. Genuine interest in flora and fauna is mandatory.

**9**

# Water Activities

- Clam Diving
- Fishing
- Kayaking
- Sailing
- Scuba Diving
- Snorkeling
- Whale Watching

Due to the unparalleled concentration and range of marine life, Jacques Cousteau nicknamed the Sea of Cortés "the world's aquarium." Here you will find a world-class location for fishing and diving. With over 800 unique species of marine life, there is always something new to see beneath the water's surface, and with tranquil, turquoise-blue water meeting white-sand beaches, the views are breathtaking from above water, too. The physical beauty of the sea as it meets the Sierra de la Giganta and the arid desert make this a truly unforgettable area to visit, so make sure you take advantage of all your water activity opportunities.

## CLAM DIVING

The beach between Loreto and Nopoló, a favorite spot for clam diving, is accessible by taking Francisco I. Madero south out of Loreto. As the street turns from pavement to dirt, follow the road as it runs parallel to the shore. You will pass a few run-down palapas. This beach is a popular vacation destination for locals on weekends, and anywhere along it is a good place to park and begin your clam hunt.

Come prepared with a flotation device, from which you can hang the clams that you collect (and float on yourself, if you choose)—this will keep you from having to hold onto a heavy bag while you are diving. The most vital equipment you will need is a snorkel and mask, as you will be face down while studying the sea floor. Be sure to slather your back with sunscreen—the blazing sun reflecting off the water can leave you scorched. (Trust us!)

Approximately twenty to thirty yards offshore, where the water is just over your head—about eight or nine feet deep—you will find two types of clams: white clams and brown ("chocolate") clams. To find a white clam you must look for two tiny black dots, or "eyes," on the sand that are a half-inch or less apart. Take a breath, dive down, and furiously dig the sand at those dots with two fingers. You should feel something hard and smooth. The white clams are pretty challenging to find at first, but compared to the chocolate clams they are a breeze. The eyes on the chocolates are not black, but, rather, a faint yellow. The two dots seem to blend right into the sand below, so it takes an immense amount of concentration to spot them and keep your eyes on them as you go under. Getting one in your hand is quite satisfying, and if you get the hang of it, you should have enough for a tasty dinner.

Put the clams on ice as soon as possible. You can either take them to a restaurant (try **Mita Gourmet** or **Tío Lupe**) or prepare them yourself. Since you went through all that effort to collect them, you might as well go with the latter.

Last but not least, clams, like oysters, are considered a natural aphrodisiac due to their high zinc content. Locals joke about the sexual potency you will get from eating clams. You'll have to see for yourself.

 **Chocolate Clams**

*Chocolatas* ("chocolate clams), named for their dark brown color, are a delicacy in Loreto. If you see them on a menu (usually as an appetizer), don't pass them up. However, the best way to enjoy these clams is to prepare them yourself. Here's how the locals do it.

Eat the clams while they are still fresh and cold. Break the shells open and spoon as much of the clam as possible from the shell—everything is edible. Instead of eating them one at a time, collect a pile of them in a bowl. Then add ketchup, lime, tomatoes, onions, and a fair amount of salt, and stir it all together into a giant glop of gastropodic goodness. It will look disgusting, but once you shovel some into your mouth on a saltine cracker you will consider making clam diving your profession.

# FISHING

If you're going fishing in Loreto, chances are the results will be favorable. Loreto is a fishing town, with a fishing culture. It is both sport and survival for the locals. The Sea of Cortés tends to get colder the farther north you go, and right where the temperature begins to change is where the fishing is the most consistent. That's Loreto. The fishing is year round, recognized mainly for the hard-fighting yellowtail in the winter and shimmering yellow and green dorado (mahi-mahi) in the summer. In fact, if dorado is what you're after, Loreto in the month of July is the best place in the world to be. Summer is also the primary season for sailfish, marlin, roosterfish, grouper, cabrilla, wahoo, and yellowfin tuna.

Before you book your fishing trip, make sure to check if your hotel has its own special fishing package or discount—most do. Still, look around, decide what kind of experience you want to have and how much you are willing to pay, and go from there. Remember, pretty much anyone with a boat can take you fishing, so don't be tempted if you come across a business card from so-and-so's fishing charter and get worried you made the wrong choice. The big name players in the Loreto fishing game are **Arturo's** and **Baja Big Fish**.

## ★ Fishing Season

| Dorado | June, July, August, September, October |
| | May, November, December |

| Marlin | June, July, August |
| | May, September |

| Roosterfish | January, February, December |
| | March, April, October, November |

| Sailfish | June, July, August, September |
| | May |

| Yellowtail | January, February, March, April |
| | May, November, December |

| Yellowfin Tuna | August, September, October |
| | July, November |

| | High Season |
| | Medium Season |

## Arturo's Sport Fishing Fleet

Arturo is the sport-fishing king. A seven-hour trip starting at six in the morning will take you to all the best spots. Arturo's fleet has fifteen different captains. All trips are insured and each boat has life vests and an emergency radio on board. Arturo's will take your order in advance and have lunches, water, and beer on board at your request. You do not have to bring anything with you if you plan ahead. On the day of your trip, you can be picked up at your hotel or the hotel nearest you. If it's easier, you can meet your captain at the marina.

Prices include 10% tax, and the option to fillet or freeze your catch. However, prices do not include pretty much everything else, such as bait (anywhere from $20 to $40 depending on the number of people), tackle (another $15 to $20), a mandatory fishing license ($12 per person), tips, food, and beverages. Arturo's offers four different types of boats, depending on the number of people in your party and what you are willing to pay. Their least expensive boat, the Super Panga, which holds one to three people, is $220; the Special Super Panga, for up to four people, is $270. The other options, the Deluxe Super Panga and the Mini-Cruiser are both $340, but offer amenities such as wider cabins, swiveling chairs, bimini shade tops, and a toilet. If you've got the dough, you can't go wrong with the mini-cruiser. This full-on motorboat has cabin space in the back only, but has a toilet in an underneath compartment and its own fighting chair. For ultimate value, try and fill your boat to capacity. The prices are set, and are no lower if you want to fish alone.

If there are fish out there, you'll catch them with Arturo. He'll send you home with something to brag about. He knows what fish are in season, where to find them, and how to reel them in. For more information, check out Arturo's snazzy website at www.arturosport.com.

*Location: On Hidalgo a half block from the Malecón*
*Hours: 9:00 a.m.-1:00 p.m., 4:00 p.m.-7:00 p.m. (Mon.–Sat.)*
*Phone: 613-135-0766*

## The Baja Big Fish Company

**Pam Bolles** started The Baja Big Fish Company more than eight years ago, and has turned it into one of the premier fishing charter services in Loreto. Baja Big Fish has intimate customer service and its number-one priority is giving customers whatever it takes to make their fishing experience fun and memorable. One of five extremely knowledgeable captains will take you out for a day of fishing, and they'll waste no time leading you straight to the prize.

Baja Big Fish also distinguishes itself from other charters by specializing in **fly-fishing**. Their **International Game Fishing Association** (IGFA)-certified weigh-station headquarters is also a pro fly shop. Choose any style of fly or have Pam place a custom order for you. Fly-fishing charters are the same price as regular charters, but rod rental is a little more expensive, with 10-, 12-, or 14-weight rods for $30 each.

Baja Big Fish offers three boat selections, a standard panga, at $240, for one or two people; a Super Panga, at $270, which holds up to three people; or a roomier Deluxe Super Panga, at $300, for three or $320 for four people. The Deluxe Super Panga comes with a bimini-style shade top, but shade tops are becoming more and more prevalent even on standard pangas. Every boat is equipped with radios and flotation and safety devices, according to regulations mandated by the port captain of Loreto. The boxed lunches (tasty turkey and avocado sandwiches on freshly-baked bread, with chips and an apple) are $8 apiece, and you can order as much water and beer as you like. A one-day Mexican fishing license will cost you $12, but one-week and one-year licenses are available too, for $32 and $55, respectively. A few more dollars for bait and rod rentals, and a three- to four-person trip will add up to a total of between $400 and $490 without tip (which is expected in the range of $10 to $20 per person).

An all-inclusive option is merely a way to ignore the hassle of add-ons and extra costs, and can be arranged for any number of days you choose. The daily rate is $322 for two people. Consider this plan if you want to pay one bill and leave the rest up to them. If you are interested, call and ask about half-day and night trips, which are offered at various times of the year.

Overall, Big Fish is a very savvy, efficient fishing company that will do what it can to help you reel in the big catch. Plus their T-shirts are very cool. Recently, Pam opened an espresso bar in her new digs so you can sit and relax and dream about the one that won't get away.

*Location: Hotel Plaza Loreto, Miguel Hidalgo*

*Phone: 613-104-0781; 613-135-1603 (Shop); 044-613-104-0781 (Cell)*

*Hours: 8:00 a.m.–5:00 p.m. (Mon.–Sat.)*

*Web: www.bajabigfish.com*

## Eco-Union Tours (at the Marina)

Based at Loreto's marina, Eco-Union Tours is a coalition of **twenty-seven local fishermen** who lead day trips and provide all the necessary fishing equipment. This is who you'll likely end up with if you show up at the marina and say you want a panga to take you out for the day with some bait and rods. The price for a Regular Panga (22-feet long, holds two people, up to seven hours) is $160; the price for a Super Panga (24-feet long, three people, up to seven hours) is $180.

In all honesty, your chances of catching a fish are probably the same with Eco-Union Tours as they are with anyone else. Four hundred dollars for a day of fishing with one of the bigger companies might seem a little too pricey for some. Consider that if the fish are biting heavily in one spot, boats from all the different companies will find their way there. By sacrificing some customer service, organization and professionalism, you can go fishing with equally knowledgeable and experienced guides for

Boats in the Loreto marina

almost half as much as the competition. So, if that works for you, these marina locals could be a good fit.

*Location: Blvd. López Mateos and A. Carrillo (Loreto Marina Office)*

*Phone: 613-135-1664*

*E-mail: ecounionadventures@hotmail.com*

## KAYAKING

Glide gracefully across the calm waters of the Sea of Cortés as you see dolphins and fish of all varieties, and maybe even the occasional whale. The Sea of Cortés is an ideal place for sea kayaking as it has a number of islands to explore, bountiful marine life, and beautiful inland views of the mountains. There are trips, ranging from several hours to several weeks, suitable to people of all skill levels. If you like kayaking, this is a can't-miss location.

## Air Temperature

| Month | Jan | Feb | Mar | Apr | May | June | July | Aug | Sept | Oct | Nov | Dec |
|-------|-----|-----|-----|-----|-----|------|------|-----|------|-----|-----|-----|
| Avg High °F | 74 | 76 | 78 | 83 | 88 | 94 | 96 | 97 | 96 | 91 | 83 | 77 |
| Avg Low °F | 50 | 50 | 52 | 55 | 61 | 69 | 76 | 77 | 75 | 68 | 58 | 62 |

## Water Temperature

| Month | Jan | Feb | Mar | Apr | May | June | July | Aug | Sept | Oct | Nov | Dec |
|-------|-----|-----|-----|-----|-----|------|------|-----|------|-----|-----|-----|
| Avg °F | 63 | 64 | 67 | 72 | 77 | 85 | 89 | 89 | 87 | 71 | 71 | 65 |

### Cormorant Dive Center

Cormorant has a fleet of high-quality plastic sea kayaks (five doubles and two singles) and offers customizable guided kayaking trips throughout the Sea of Cortés. The trips run year round except for the summer months, when the heat limits the trips to a maximum of three hours. The most popular trip goes from just north of Loreto's marina to **Isla Coronado**, but the guides are flexible. They even have an air-conditioned van that can take you to **Puerto Escondido** for a different launching point. Cormorant can also arrange long multi-day kayaking trips, as long as you have a minimum of four people in your group.

*Location: Paseo Hidalgo between Colegio and Pino Suárez*

*Hours: 8:00 a.m.–8:00 p.m.*

*Phone: 613-135-2140*

*Web: www.loretours.com*

### Paddling South

The "pioneers" of Baja kayaking, Paddling South is definitely *the* place to go for kayaking. Run by **Trudi Angell**, who has kayaked the area for over thirty years, this operation specializes in multi-day trips all across the Baja peninsula.

Although day trips are not the main emphasis of Paddling South, if you give Trudi 24-hour's notice she can organize a two- to three-hour English-speaking guided kayaking trip during the day or at sunset, with instruction for beginners. The prices start at $35 for a Loreto beach departure. If you would like to kayak from a more remote location, discuss pricing with Trudi.

Multi-day kayaking trips are available throughout the year and range from $995 for an eight-day trip to $1,295 for a fourteen-day trip, the latter of which will take you from **Agua Verde** all the way to **La Paz**. Some kayak trips include whale watching. The trips are preplanned, so check the trip schedule on the website and contact Paddling South well in advance to check availability and to make your initial $200 deposit. There are several weeks each season that Trudi leaves unscheduled to accommodate for customizable trips, so if you have a private group you can probably arrange something. Every guide has lived in the area, is bilingual, and is extremely experienced in local lore and naturalist information. The prices include food, camping supplies, and everything else you will need on the trip.

*Phone: 800-398-6200, 707-942-4550*
*Fax: 707-942-8017*
*E-mail: info@tourbaja.com*
*Web: www.tourbaja.com*

## SAILING

Sailing is the perfect way to explore the majestic Sea of Cortés in a boat more comfortable than a fishing panga. Set sail and relax as you glide through the blue waters, and explore the hidden coves and turquoise harbors of Loreto's marine park. If you have time, hoist the canvas and head north to **Bahía Concepción**, considered one of the most beautiful bays in the region. Anchor your boat and go for a swim; grab some snorkel equipment so you can observe the underwater life of the surrounding islands. If you're on the water long enough, you might be lucky enough to find schools of dolphin or blue whales in their natural habitat.

# Sailing/Day Trips

## Velas de Loreto

Velas is the owner of **El Don**, a 65-foot triple-cabin yacht. They offer half-day cruises around the Loreto marine park from 8:00 a.m. to noon or 1:00 p.m. to 5:00 p.m., for $65 per person. Snacks are included, but guests should bring their own equipment if they plan to snorkel. A full day, 9:00 a.m. to 4:00 p.m., costs $110 per person. Two-hour sunset cruises are available for $45 per person. You can turn your day on the water into an ecotour by looking for blue or fin whales and observing the abundant marine life. El Don holds up to twenty-five passengers. The Mexican crew can also serve you on either a private overnight charter or a multi-day trip (prices vary).

Velas de Loreto is recommended for those who simply want to cruise in luxury. Charter El Don to ride in style for the day with a large group. However, you'll want to look to the BajaSail catamaran if longer ecotourism and adventure activities are more suitable for you. Visit their website to view photographs of El Don.

*Location: Fco. I. Madero and Benito Juárez, Col. Centro*

*Phone: 613-135-1247*

*E-mail: info@velasdeloreto.com; reservations@velasdeloreto.com*

*Web: www.velasdeloreto.com*

# Sailing/Multi-Day Trips

## BajaSail.Net

BajaSail has a 47-foot luxury catamaran that goes by the same name and can sleep up to eight guests. BajaSail offers week-long all-inclusive adventure tours. Each day of the trip is preplanned, and activities such as whale watching, scuba diving, snorkeling, hiking, and kayaking are included in your itinerary. You will sail south to **Isla Danzante**, make stops at **Carmen** and **Coronado** Islands, head north to **Mulegé** to see some cave paintings, sail through **Bahía Concepción**, and finally head back to Loreto. Three meals per day are included, and are either served on board or at select restaurants on the shore closest to where you anchor. The package also includes one night at the **Inn at Loreto Bay**. The all-inclusive price for the week per person is $1,925. If you choose to sail solo, you will be required to pay an $800 supplementary fee, so try to find a friend to travel with you. Note that all participants must purchase their own travel insurance and show proof of insurance prior to boarding.

BajaSail also offers short three-hour half-day trips and full-day trips to **Isla Danzante**, as well as sunset cruises, all on a smaller catamaran. Prices vary based on the number of people. The crew is composed of naturalists, trained tour guides, and sailing aficionados. BajaSail is a responsible charter service with your safety and your satisfaction always in mind.

*Phone: 760-804-5788*
*Fax: 760-603-0569*
*E-mail: info@bajasail.net*
*Web: www.bajasail.net*

## Sailing Baja

**Trudi Angell** runs Paddling South, Pedaling South, and Saddling South, while her partner, **Douglas Knapp**, is in charge of the sailing branch of the company, Sailing Baja. Doug has been running a learn-to-sail program for twenty-three years—a five-day course with instruction on a Catalina 22. Upon completion, each student is awarded a **Small Boat Sailor Certification** from the **United States Sailing Association**. The cost is $525 per student, with lunch included on board each day. Courses are offered once a month when sailing is at its best, November–May. Since the training is limited to two to four people, check the course dates for each month online at www.tourbaja.com and book in advance.

Also, qualified sailors can rent the Catalina 22 on bareboat charters. With no captain on board, cruise with up to four people on multi-day trips and anchor whenever or wherever you choose. The cost is $825 for one week. Contact Doug to apply for the charter, set dates, and explain your sailing experience. Sailing Baja is the only charter in Loreto that offers bareboat trips. Avid sailors eager to take the helm, look no further.

On their larger, 27-foot catamaran, five-day guided cruises are available for four to six guests. Explore the islands, sleep on the beach, snorkel, and enjoy the wildlife on these customizable sailing adventures. The base price is $995 per person. In order to reserve your spot on these multi-day excursions, a $200 per person deposit is requested.

Trudi and Douglas are truly experts in ecotourism, priding themselves on their many years of experience. With day trips and sunset cruises in the lineup, the well-rounded Sailing Baja offers a little bit of everything.

*Phone: 800-398-6200, 707-942-4550*

*Fax: 707-942-8017*

*E-mail: info@tourbaja.com*

*Web: www.tourbaja.com*

## SCUBA DIVING

The Sea of Cortés is home to some of the best scuba diving on earth. While its claim to fame is the presence of the extremely rare **Humboldt**

### ⭐ HUMBOLDT SQUID

There have been numerous articles written and years of research done on the Humboldt squid in the Sea of Cortés. Surprisingly, there is still little known about some of the aspects of this fascinating creature. Stories about their behavior show they range from being docile to very curious to aggressive. With a reputation that spans these extremes, the truth is probably somewhere in the middle, but divers should always err to the cautious side.

Humboldt squid live in deep water—up to 2,300 ft.—in the east side of the Pacific from Tierra del Fuego north into the Sea of Cortés. Some have appeared as far north as Alaska. They take their name from the Humboldt Current that extends from northern Peru to Southern Chile. It is generally thought they have a relatively short life span of about one year, although some researchers think possibly up to four years, and they reproduce only once. These awesome animals can reach over 6ft + (2m+) in length and weigh as much as 100 lbs. (45kg). Their color varies from red to white and, like other cephalopods, muscle-bound chromatophores on their skin enable them to flash these undulating colors in rhythmic waves, a behavior believed to be part of a complex communication system.

Unlike the octopus, squid have two additional long tentacles with 'pads' at the tips to reach out and capture food, while they use the other eight tentacles to manipulate the catch into their beak-like mouth. They can move extremely fast (15 miles per hour) with instant reverse by ejecting water through a siphon and using two triangular-shaped fins. Since they grow to such a large size so rapidly, they are voracious eaters and tend to be aggressive and very competitive. They are also cannibalistic and will eat other injured squid. One study showed that over 26% of 500 squids whose stomachs were checked

**squid** and the world's largest fish, the whale shark, it is also a fabulous destination for simple recreational dives. The dive sites are scarp (slopes caused by erosion) and underwater boulders, and while each of them offers unique conditions, they all have an abundance of tropical fish species, and plenty of large grouper and sea turtles. Blacktip sharks and hammerheads patrol the sea, as well as manta rays and spotted eagle rays. On a lucky day, you may even witness schools of three-meter mobula (similar to manta rays), one of the most surreal sights one can see as a diver. Whales and dolphins round out the collection of marine life. The visibility ranges from about 30–130 ft (10–40 m), and the water temperature ranges from 60–89 degrees Fahrenheit depending on the month.

had other squid remnants inside! They stay deep in the daytime and come shallower at night to feed. They hunt in large schools that contain as many as 1,200 individuals.

What preys on the Humboldt squid? Sperm and pilot whales, sharks, sea lions, and billfish are their natural enemies. But humans are their largest predator, in growing numbers for the commercial industry of calamari. Normally, these squid have a slightly ammonia/acidic flavor which makes them not so tasty to other marine creatures, but this is processed out for commercial consumption.

There have been confirmed reports of divers and fishermen being attacked by Humboldt squid in open water. Each of the suction cups on their tentacles has a set of teeth or barbs which aid them in grabbing their prey. These barbs will draw blood on human skin. This characteristic coupled with their beak tends to add to their reputation to be dangerous, especially in the right circumstances. Even bringing one onto a boat can be a formidable experience. Shooting gallons of water, ink, and grabbing anything within reach creates quite an experience for a first-time encounter with these incredible creatures.

But as with all animals, they do not attack maliciously, as we humans like to make out as we sensationalize and glamorize our stories. They are just another co-inhabitant sharing our planet. Being no different than any other living creature, they have only one thing on their minds—survival.

*Bruce Williams, Dolphin Dive Center*

See color photograph of a Humboldt squid on page 6.

## Cormorant Dive Center

Cormorant is **SSI affiliated and certified** with all the necessary park permits. They are fully insured and service the dive tanks yearly and the other equipment every eighteen months. They have their own compressor and a large supply of top-quality equipment, including various buoyancy control devices (BCDs) to suit your diving level. There are two dive instructors and four dive masters to take you out, but we recommend **Juve Orozco**, an extremely dedicated and knowledgeable instructor who is bound to give you a great experience.

Cormorant offers three main dive trips. Each trip goes for roughly six hours and includes two tanks, lunch, drinks, and park fees. You will need to pay $30 for a full set of equipment if you do not have your own. There is a minimum of three people required for each trip. The prices are per person. **Coronado** is $79, the trip to **Carmen** is $89, and the **Danzante** trip is $99; price differences are based on travel distances to the islands. If you get a larger group, the price per person may go down.

*Location: On Miguel Hidalgo between Colegio and Pino Suárez*

*Hours: 8:00 a.m.–8:00 p.m.*

*Phone: 613-135-2140*

*Web: www.loretours.com*

## Dolphin Dive Center

Dolphin Dive Center is the premier dive outfitter in Loreto. As the only shop associated with the **Professional Association of Diving Instructors** (PADI) rather than Scuba Schools International (SSI), Dolphin is the only place to go to if you want dive certifications that will be accepted around the world. It sets the standard in terms of professionalism, safety, and knowledge. It is owned by **Bruce Williams**, **Susan Speck**, and **Javier Lopez**. **Rafael Murillo**, a local Mexican dive master, is the general manager. The staff is extremely proficient and helpful.

Bruce meticulously maintains all of the equipment, servicing the tanks yearly. He makes sure everything in his possession is of the highest standards and rents out full sets of scuba gear for $40 per day or $140 for a week. Call for pricing on individual pieces of equipment.

All day trips generally last from 8:30 a.m. to 2:30 p.m. Dolphin has its own compressor, insurance, and every permit there is, and they use every safety precaution. All prices are per person and include equipment.

There are no discounts based on larger groups. Trip packages include: **Isla Coronado**, $89; **Isla del Carmen**, $99; **Isla Danzante**, $105; the **Mine Sweeper shipwreck**, $105; and a night dive (four people minimum, may be negotiable), $65. The Open Water Diver class costs $400 and Specialist Courses cost $150. Dolphin also offers a number of other PADI courses if you are in need of more specific training.

*Location: A block from the Marina on Benito Juárez*
*Hours: 9:00 a.m.–1:00 p.m., 5:00 p.m.–7:00 p.m.*
*Phone: 613-135-1914*
*Web: www.dolphindivebaja.com*

# SNORKELING

Although there are no trips specifically designed for just snorkeling, it is an option as part of any of the island day trips. A number of outfitters run combination snorkel and island-exploration trips in which they will guide you to **Coronado**, **Carmen**, or **Danzante** islands. You can then choose to do whatever you want, be it snorkeling, hiking on the islands, or lazing on the beach.

## Cormorant Dive Center

Cormorant offers fully-insured and certified six-hour excursions to **Coronado**, **Carmen**, or **Danzante** Islands. They know the area well, and will make sure you get the most out of your snorkeling experience by taking you to the best drop spots. Each trip is slightly customizable, and a guide will be assigned to your group who is suited to your primary interests. While some guides specialize in naturalist hikes and others in snorkeling, they are all capable in every area. English-speaking guides are available upon request. The prices are per person and based on a three-person minimum. Larger groups may lower the per-person prices. The prices include lunch, drinks, park permits, and snorkel equipment. Coronado costs $55; Carmen and Danzante are each $65.

*Location: On Miguel Hidalgo between Colegio and Pino Suárez*
*Hours: 8:00 a.m.–8:00 p.m.*
*Phone: 613-135-2140*
*Web: www.loretours.com*

### Dolphin Dive Center

Dolphin offers certified trips with English-speaking guides to **Isla Coronado** for $55 per person with a three-person minimum. If you request a snorkel/island trip to one of the other islands, they will work something out for you. The prices include lunch and equipment. The snorkel trips are built into the island trips, so some members of your group can spend time exploring Isla Coronado with a trained guide while others snorkel. Dolphin is fully insured, carries medical and first-aid equipment, and has all of the necessary park permits. Their knowledge of marine life and best snorkel areas makes them a great choice.

*Location: A block from the Marina on Benito Juárez*

*Hours: 9:00 a.m.–1:00 p.m., 5:00 p.m.–7:00 p.m.*

*Phone: 613-135-1914*

*Web: www.dolphindivebaja.com*

## WHALE WATCHING

While the waters of Loreto's marine park get their fair share of blue, fin, sperm, minke, sei, pilot, orca, and humpback whales, watchers must travel to **Bahía Magdalena**, on the west coast of the Baja peninsula, for the biggest reward, the grey whale. The grey whales migrate up to 6,000 miles (9,656 km) from the Bering Sea in Alaska, and then settle into Magdalena Bay to reproduce, nurse, and feed their young from January to March. It is often reported that whales surface close enough to your boat that you can reach down and pet them. The outfitters in Loreto can arrange trips for you to the Pacific side with transportation included. Or you could drive yourself to Magdalena Bay and hire a guide there—they are plentiful.

Friendly Grey Whale

For those who wish to remain in Loreto, you will have to settle for the world's largest mammal: the 100-foot blue whale, weighing in at a modest 150 tons. Finback whales are also present, but move faster than the blue whale and thus are more difficult to follow. Grey whales are more rare, but the entire Sea of Cortés is within their possible range. If you're in Loreto in the wintertime, make whale watching a priority.

## C&C Tours and Ground Services

From December 15 to early/mid April (depending on the whale migration), C&C Tours offers full day whale-watching excursions to **López Mateos at Bahía Magdalena**, across the Baja peninsula from Loreto. The trips go from 7:30 a.m. to 5:00 p.m. and include transportation in an air-conditioned van, a bilingual naturalist guide, lunch, and best of all, a full-lobster dinner. C&C, like all other outfitters who lead trips to the Pacific Ocean, rents boats from another party. Although their trips are not insured, in over twenty years of whale-watching tours with more than 1,400 people last year alone, they have never had any safety issues. C&C is a reliable tour company that delivers what they promise. Prices are $150 per person, with a four-person minimum.

*Location: Misión de San Ignacio, Nopoló*

*Phone: 613-133-0151*

## Cormorant Dive Center

The same four naturalist guides who lead diving, biking, and kayaking expeditions for Cormorant also run the whale-watching tours. **Juve**, the lead guide, and the remainder of his guide staff, are expert whale observers. They know where to find every kind of whale out there. With a minimum of two people, seven-hour excursions are offered for blue and fin whales, found January through April in Loreto Bay, located on the far side of **Isla del Carmen**. Cormorant can also take you to **Bahía Magdalena** to view grey whales. Round-trip transportation is included for a minimum of three persons. Your panga captain will strategically steer you to the best position for viewing the magnificent creatures when they surface. If you're lucky, you might even get close enough to actually touch one. All trips cost $130 per person, with tax and lunch included.

*Location: On Miguel Hidalgo between Colegio and Pino Suárez*

*Hours: 8:00 a.m.–8:00 p.m.*

*Phone: 613-135-2140*

*Web: www.loretours.com*

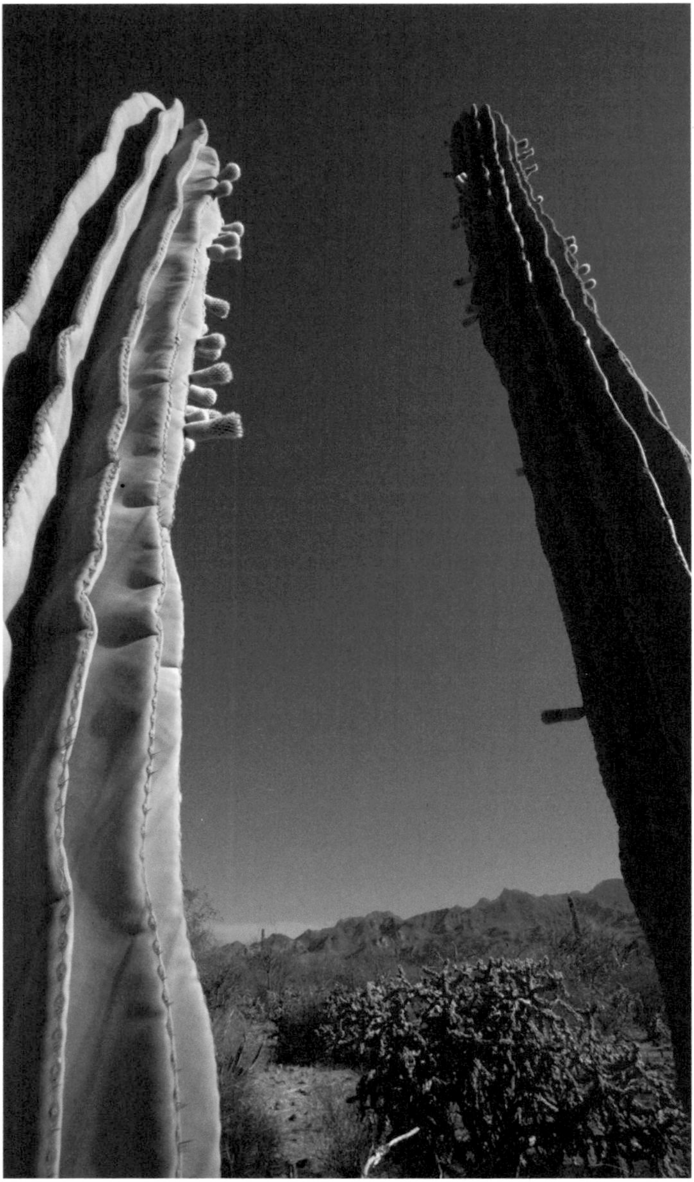

Photo by Doug Ogle

# Land Activities

- ATV Rentals
- Cave Paintings
- Customizable Mountain Excursions
- Golf
- Hiking
- Horseback Riding
- Mountain Biking/Day Trips
- Mountain Biking/Multi-Day Trips
- Tennis

# ATV RENTALS

### Cormorant Dive Center

Cormorant owns seven 2006-model Honda ATVs—two 500cc support vehicles and five 350cc vehicles—for tourists. Cormorant's fully insured ATV trips are very similar to their mountain-biking trips, with day excursions to either **Primer Agua** ($65 per person, tax included) or **San Javier** ($90 per person). The San Javier ride takes you beyond the historic mission to a local ranch. The jagged, winding terrain will make for an exciting adventure and plenty of scenic vistas. Snacks and drinks are included in the prices listed above. There is a two-person minimum.

*Location: On Miguel Hidalgo between Colegio and Pino Suárez*

*Hours: 8:00 a.m.–8:00 p.m.*

*Phone: 613-135-2140*

*Web: www.loretours.com*

# CAVE PAINTINGS

### Cormorant Dive Center

If you are interested in seeing the beautiful and historic regional cave paintings, the best sites are in the foothills just to the west of **Mulegé**, north of Loreto. Cormorant will take you to two ideal cave-painting locations about an hour away from town called **"La Pinguica"** and **"Tres Marías."** The route is part highway and part dirt roads, and the drive takes seven hours. Bring sturdy shoes because some hiking is involved. The cost is $119 per person, with a three-person minimum. Cormorant is a safe bet. Their naturalist guides know all the secrets of the terrain and they have an air-conditioned GMC Suburban that travels the roads and keeps you comfortable.

*Location: On Miguel Hidalgo between Colegio and Pino Suárez*

*Hours: 8:00 a.m.–8:00 p.m.*

*Phone: 613-135-2140*

*Web: www.loretours.com*

## Kuyimá

Kuyimá is a "100% Mexican company, dedicated to the development of ecotourism" in the area, with a focus on sustainable development. They offer day trips and multi-day trips, mostly to the **Sierra de San Francisco** cave paintings (as well as whale watching trips) and have educational summer camps for kids. Their office is in **San Ignacio**.

*Location: At the front of the plaza on the side opposite the Mission—Morelos #23, on the corner of Hidalgo St. (San Ignacio)*

*E-mail: kuyima@prodigy.net.mx*

*Web: www.kuyima.com/cave/index.html*

## Saddling South

**Trudi Angell**, with twenty years of traveling the peninsula by mule and trail, offers multi-day pack and hike trips to favorite rock art sites. More than a tour, her adventures show you the culture and soul of the people of the sierra as local cowboy singers and musicians add to the ambiance. *(See sidebar on page 172–173.)*

*Phone: 800-398-6200 (U.S. Office)*

*E-mail: info@tourbaja.com*

*Web: www.TourBaja.com*

# CUSTOMIZABLE MOUNTAIN EXCURSIONS

Many secrets are kept within the peaks and valleys of the **Sierra de la Giganta**. If you just want to go exploring or hike through the terrain with a knowledgeable local guide, you can surely be accommodated. A customizable mountain excursion can be designed for you. Here are our recommendations.

## Adventure Baja

**Kathy Hill**, a gringo who lives in Loreto and the founder of Adventure Baja, will not only show you all the secret treasures hidden within the **Sierra de la Giganta**, she will gladly customize your excursion to match your personal preferences. Ranches, churches, flora and fauna, rock formations, canyons, cave paintings, hiking, bird watching—anything you

The Great Mural Rock Art of the Sierra San Francisco is a cultural treasure hidden in the heart of Baja California, Mexico. Scarcely a decade has passed since several important sites were designated World Heritage quality, and they have recently become more accessible to adventure travelers. Today, Cueva El Ratón can be reached in a high-clearance vehicle, El Palmarito by a two-hour drive off of Mexican Highway 1 and a two-hour hike to the site, and Cueva Pintada and Cueva de las Flechas via a minimum two-day trek into Santa Teresa Canyon. Many other sites require some extensive planning to visit, but offer an amazing experience as you explore the old trails of the Baja California peninsula.

In 1993, UNESCO and Mexico's agency, National Institute of Anthropology and History (INAH), began a program to protect and organize access to the remote archeological sites. Ranchers from the local villages have been authorized by INAH and are available to lead tourists to the rock art. However, it takes a bit of prior planning.

### Sierra San Francisco Do-It-Yourself

*General Information*
Best season October through May; to access, you'll need vehicle with high clearance (but not necessarily four-wheel drive). Some Spanish is very helpful. Take food and water with you; use minimum-impact desert travel techniques *(www.lnt.org/programs/lnt7/index.html)* at *www.leavenotrace.org*.

*Travel*
*Driving:* On Mexico Highway 1, drive to the town of San Ignacio, about 550 miles south of the Tijuana border. Flying/Driving: Fly into Loreto from Los Angeles or the Southwest, and then rent a vehicle, hire a taxi, or take a bus north to San Ignacio, about a four-hour trip. From

Paintings at Cueva de las Flechas. See color photos on page 140.
©Saddling South, www.TourBaja.com

San Ignacio you can drive or hire a taxi van and go to either village—San Francisco de la Sierra or Santa Marta—to view a protected rock art "gallery," or to access the trailheads for an extended visit.

*Tours and Guides*

For a relatively quick glimpse (one full day) you can visit Cueva El Ratón (San Francisco de la Sierra)—worth a visit if you have never seen mural art and prefer not to hike. Or you can try Cueva Palmarito (Santa Marta), very much worth a visit if you have never seen mural rock art and are able to hike or ride a mule for about three hours round trip.

For a three- or four-day trek—the best trip for a minimum amount of time—visit two major sites, La Pintada and Las Flechas, and have access to a possible six other sites.

From San Ignacio, check in at the INAH office, drive two hours to San Francisco de la Sierra, meet the guides and pack animals/riding animals, hike three to five hours to camp, and spend a day or two visiting sites. Rugged and steep trails take you down into Santa Teresa Canyon where camping sites are designated and water is available but needs to be treated. No campfires are permitted at canyon sites. Take all personal camping gear, cooking gear, and enough food to share with local guides. The cost comes to about $65 per person per day for fees, guide, pack animal, and riding animal (varies with size of group and number of riding animals desired) and does not include your travel expenses, cost of food, or tips. Best to have some Spanish language ability.

*Trudi Angell, Saddling South, Pedaling South, Paddling South*

Saddling South, www.TourBaja.com
Kuyima (based in San Ignacio), www.Kuyima.com

## Meet Kathy!

When you're visiting Loreto, **Kathleen "Kathy" Hill** is the lady to meet. She runs many unique businesses out of the same office. Located just past the main stoplight on Miguel Hidalgo, her store, Gecko's, is filled with beautiful hand-crafted stone jewelry and other arts and crafts, a truly one-of-a-kind collection. The shop is wonderfully decorated, with a small kitchen in the back. Kathy offers a "food-to-go" catering service, with items like soup, stew, and potato salad. Her thirst for adventure and true passion for Baja led to the creation of Adventure Baja, an adventure tourism company she runs with her partner, Hector Ramirez.

Kathy is the ultimate resource for English- and Spanish-speaking visitors alike. Look around her store and you'll find Baja Magazine and various informative brochures, as well as a buy-and-sell board where anyone can post ads for the "junk" they are trying to get rid of. She's been around, and knows the region well. She can tell you what's really happening on the local scene. Kathy is definitely someone worth meeting and a great person to chat with about your miscellaneous Baja- or Loreto-specific questions. As Kathy says, "Just look for the blue doors on Miguel Hidalgo."

want to do, Kathy can take you there (all meals included). Her experience in the catering business makes her perfect for organizing homemade traditional dinners with hospitable rancheros. She charges $85 per person per trip and deals mostly with groups of four or more people. If you have less than four, don't fret, Kathy is always willing to work out a solution and negotiate a fair price. She hires taxis to make all of the excursions and the cost of transportation is included. If you aren't set on one particular sport or activity, turn to Adventure Baja, perfect for families and big groups. Persons of all ages are welcome.

*Location: Her storefront, Gecko's, Salvatierra and Emiliano Zapata*

*Phone: 613-135-2505*

*E-mail: adventurebaja@yahoo.com*

## Cormorant Dive Center

Naturalist and expert guide **Juve** loves to take people into the mountains and teach them about indigenous culture, history, desert survival tactics, plant and animal species, and all the secrets of the arroyos. If you simply want to spend the day exploring the mountains, you can absolutely do

Photo by Doug Ogle

so without a mountain bike or without going all the way to San Javier. There are plenty of hidden canyons and trails waiting for you, and Cormorant knows them all. Talk to either Juve or **Victor** at Cormorant and be specific about your areas of interest. Since the trips are customizable, the prices vary, and are negotiable but reasonable.

*Location: Miguel Hidalgo between Colegio and Pino Suárez*

*Hours: 8:00 a.m.–8:00 p.m.*

*Phone: 613-135-2140*

*Web: www.loretours.com*

## GOLF

The 18-hole, par 72, 5,400-yard **Campo de Golf Loreto** course is currently being redesigned by **2001 British Open Champion David Duval**, and construction has begun by the **Loreto Bay Company** for the installation of a PGA-quality golf course and clubhouse. It will be operated by **Troon Golf of Scottsdale, Arizona**. In keeping with the Loreto Bay Company's commitment to sustainable development, the golf course is being planted with ecofocused, saltwater-irrigable paspalum grass.

Currently, the back nine incorporates shallow, mangrove-lined estuaries—natural extensions of the surrounding habitat—that make for a multitude of challenging over-water shots with extraordinary views. The 14th is the most noteworthy hole, with jaw-dropping views of the waterways and the Sea of Cortés, not to mention a tee-shot that will test your skills big-time. Two lakes and plenty of bunkers round out the obstacles. The new course is expected to be a stunning, world-class upgrade to this beautifully laid out course. Stay tuned for details.

## HIKING

Many tour operators include hiking as a component of the excursions they offer to the nearby islands or to **San Javier Mission**. Horseback riding tours, mountain biking tours, and cave-painting trips usually also include hiking. However,

©Saddling South, www.TourBaja.com

hiking-only tours are becoming more prevalent in the Loreto area, and some outfitters have started to accommodate the nature-loving crowd. Although hiking solo is an option, it is dangerous and not recommended.

### C&C Tours and Ground Services

C&C Tours offers hikes to a popular trekking destination known as **Tabor Canyon** near **Puerto Escondido**. To ensure that you have two hands free at all time to navigate the rocky terrain, you will bring very little with you—only water and fresh veggies are included. The price per person is $35, but the per-person rates increase for groups that do not meet the six-person minimum. Two naturalist guides will accompany you on the best route for scenic views and fun early-morning exercise. Other hikes are offered to the oases and arroyos in the mountain foothills, with an emphasis on flora, fauna, and wildlife. There is a daily tour from 6:30 a.m. to 8:30 a.m., with a discounted $22 per person rate.

*Location: Misión de San Ignacio, Nopoló*

*Phone: 613-133-0151*

# HORSEBACK RIDING

Feel the wind rush through your hair as you gallop across Loreto's charming beaches as the sun sets over the tranquil Sea of Cortés, or take a ride through the **Sierra de la Giganta** foothills, trotting among the desert's mountain reptiles and cacti. Horseback riding is a great way to experience the natural beauty of the Loreto area, and there are excursions appropriate for the avid adventurer as well as those who enjoy a more leisurely romantic ride. Make sure you go to the correct outfitter to suit your personal interests.

### Pancho's Horseback Riding

Pancho runs a very informal horseback riding operation. He has five horses, and will take groups on rides along the beach or into the mountains for $15 per hour. Day trips to **San Javier** with a support truck that carries lunch and water, included in the price, last 15 hours and cost $300 per person. If you have more than two people, the cost may drop to $200. Multi-day trips can also be arranged but are certainly not recommended here as he is not set up with the appropriate amenities of other professional multi-day trips. Recommended only for short rides down the beach.

*Location: On beach in front of the Oasis Hotel at far South end of the Malecón*

## Saddling South

The premier horseback riding operation, Saddling South, is run by **Trudi Angell**. She offers a number of incredible multi-day horseback and mule riding trips all over the Baja peninsula. Every trip has a different theme. Some focus on visiting traditional Mexican ranches, others go through the sugarcane villages or to spectacular cave paintings. Some specialize in naturalist information on flora and fauna. Trudi accompanies every trip, along with one or two other specialty guides.

A list of trips and dates are available on the Saddling South website at www.tourbaja.com. Generally the trips last about a week and cost about $1,000. Prices are all inclusive, so you will not need to worry about accommodations or food. You will need to book your trip and pay the $200 deposit well in advance because the excursions are very popular and fill up quickly. Customizable trips are also available. If you are interested call Trudi and discuss the logistics.

To arrange for a day trip when you are visiting Loreto it is best to contact Trudi well in advance via the numbers or email listed below. Trudi is often out on tours, but with advance planning you might get lucky and be able to join her on a very informative day ride in the Loreto area.

*Phone: 800-398-6200; 707-942-4550*

*Fax: 707-942-8017*

*E-mail: info@tourbaja.com*

*Web: www.tourbaja.com*

Trudi Angell of Saddling South with her pal Mora out on a week-long rock art trip.

©Paddling South. www.TourBaja.com

Ride high-desert back roads in the Sierra
de la Giganta.

Hikers take a break at a hidden oases
near Loreto.

On a Saddling South trip, riders prepare to settle in for the night in a camp three days to the north of
the Sierra de San Francisco.

Chuckwalla

©Jack Swenson, www.BajaPhotos.com

San Gregorio Cave Paintings

Cueva de Las Flechas Cave Paintings

Brown Pelican, Breeding Plumage

Snowy Egret 141

Turkey Vultures

Belted Kingfisher

Magnificent Frigatebird

Reddish Egret

Yellow-footed Gull with Octopus. (This is a gull species that is only found in the
Gulf of California, it's one of several endemic seabirds in the gulf region.)

Black-Throated Sparrow

Hooded Oriole

Gila Woodpecker

Acorn Woodpecker

Cassin's Kingbird

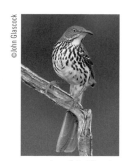

Long-Tailed Thrasher

Xantus' Hummingbird

Verdin

**143**

Matacora (Limberbush)

Uña de Gato (Cat's Claw)

Palo Blanco

Punta de Flecha (Arrowweed)

Torote Colorado (Elephant Tree)

Lomboy Blanco (Ashy Limberbush)

All photographs
on this page
by Doug Ogle

144

Photo by Doug Ogle

**Cecilia Fischer**, a naturalist with the Loreto Bay Foundation and a local Loretana, identifies six plants and their special properties that could keep you alive (or at least smelling good) in case you find yourself stranded in the desert.

*Matacora:* The dye from this "limberbush" is utilized for making the cave art that can be found on the outskirts of Loreto. Native people also use it for basket weaving, and for stitching wounds. Matacora is unique because its fibers dissolve in your blood. (The agave plant also has fibers that dissolve in the blood but, to avoid infection, its needle must be burned to deactivate a toxin when stitching wounds).

*Uña de Gato:* This "cat's claw" is named after the curved thorns on its branches. Its ground bark is believed to help boost the immune system, stop nosebleed, and even stimulate weight loss. Too good to be true?

*Palo Blanco:* This beautiful white tree has a deep taproot, and is hard to miss. Historically, its bark was stripped and used for dyeing clothes made from mule or deer hides, which were then tanned with caliche (lime).

*Punta de Flecha:* This acidic "arrowweed" bush is the one you don't want to touch when you are hiking through the desert. No animals want to touch it, either, which is why it usually has all of its leaves intact.

*Torote Colorado:* This rare type of "elephant tree," named after its curving stalk, is extremely aromatic. Its primary use is for incense. The smell this tree emits is hard to pinpoint, but most people agree that it smells pretty good.

*Lomboy Blanco:* Lomboy, or Ashy Limberbush, is the natural Band-Aid. The sticky goo from this sun-loving shrub can be used to protect cuts and scrapes, which, in the desert, can be plentiful.

# MOUNTAIN BIKING/DAY TRIPS

## Cormorant Dive Center

Cormorant is one of the first places to turn to if you are interested in mountain biking. They own fifteen sturdy **Mongoose** mountain bikes and offer day trips to nearby **Primer Agua Oasis** ($55 per person, tax included) as well as six- or seven-day trips across the peninsula to the Pacific Ocean. If you desire, you can bike all the way to **Misión San Javier**, a 22-mile (36-km) ride ($123 per person). **Juve**, a very experienced and knowledgeable tour guide, or one of his trained English-speaking guides will lead your trip. On your way you will learn about the flora and fauna and some desert survival techniques. You'll stop to hike through **Las Parras Canyon** and visit **Rancho Las Parras**, where you will experience the ranchero lifestyle. Cormorant is very respectful of the land and does not tread on privately-owned property without permission. All trips include lunch and soft drinks. There is a two-person minimum.

*Location: On Miguel Hidalgo between Colegio and Pino Suárez*

*Hours: 8:00 a.m.–8:00 p.m.*

*Phone: 613-135-2140*

*Web: www.loretours.com*

# MOUNTAIN BIKING/MULTI-DAY TRIPS

## Pedaling South

Pedaling South is owned by **Trudi Angell**. Trudi specializes in multi-day trips, usually lasting eight days. Every rider will be equipped with a Trek or Novara mountain bike. Feel free to bring your own. Tents and other supplies are included, so all you need to bring with you is clothing and a sleeping bag. All equipment will be carried in a support vehicle, and anyone is welcomed to take a break from biking when they choose. Meals will be provided and prepared by your knowledgeable, bilingual guide. Trudi puts extra emphasis on including the local people, experiencing their culture and learning about their history, so you will visit local ranches and enjoy home-cooked recipes from friendly, traditional farmers. Pedaling South can accommodate most special requests, so feel free to discuss ways to customize your trips to cater to your strengths or personal preferences.

Trudi's mountain biking/sea kayaking combo trips are a popular choice for those who want it all. In fall and winter fully catered eight-day combo trips are based in quaint B&B bungalows in the village of San Javier, and the kayaking section is a beach basecamp with day trips to islands and coastal beaches. In spring 2008 a new venue is being offered with the mountain B&B plus a beach retreat, for a kayak base with more ammenities. REI Adventures also books multisport tours with Pedaling South for several weeks each season, and you may contact Trudi to arrange private day trips, combos, and multiday all-mountain bike tours for avid bikers, groups or biking clubs. See the Pedaling South combo trip itinerary on www.TourBaja.com for more information.

*Phone: 800 398-6200, 707-942-4550*
*Fax: 707-942-8017*
*E-mail: info@tourbaja.com*
*Web: www.tourbaja.com*

# TENNIS

**The Loreto Bay Company** also purchased the **Centro Tenístico de Loreto**, originally designed and dedicated by **John McEnroe**, and the company plans a major renovation of it. Currently, the center has eight professional lighted courts and a championship tennis stadium that holds up to 250 spectators. Each court has its own garden area attached. As the Loreto Bay development in **Nopoló** continues to expand, it will no longer be common to drive past a vacant facility. It is destined to become a major sports attraction in the area.

*Hours: 8:00 a.m.–6:00 p.m. (Mon.–Fri.); 9:00 a.m.–5:00 p.m. (Weekends)*
*Phone: 613-133-0788 or 613-133-0129*

## ★ Danzante Bird Checklist

| CLASS AND BIRD NAME | Spring | Summer | Fall | Winter |
|---|---|---|---|---|
| Eared Grebe | | X | | |
| Red-Billed Tropicbird[1] | X | X | X | X |
| Brown Pelican | X | X | X | X |
| Blue-Footed Booby[1] | X | X | X | X |
| Brown Booby[1] | | X | | |
| Double-Crested Cormorant | X | X | X | X |
| Magnificent Frigatebird | X | X | X | X |
| Great Blue Heron | X | X | X | X |
| Great Egret | | | X | X |
| Snowy Egret | X | X | X | X |
| Reddish Egret | X | X | X | X |
| Turkey Vulture | X | X | X | X |
| Osprey | X | X | X | X |
| Red-Tailed Hawk | X | X | X | X |
| Sharp-Shinned Hawk | | | | X |
| American Kestrel | X | X | X | X |
| California Quail | | X | | |
| Spotted Sandpiper | | | | X |
| Western Sandpiper | | | X | X |
| Red-Necked Phalarope | | | X | X |
| Yellow-Footed Gull | | X | | |
| Heermann's Gull | X | | | X |
| Royal Tern | | | X | X |
| Common Ground Dove | X | X | X | X |
| White-Winged Dove | X | X | X | X |
| Greater Roadrunner | X | X | X | X |
| Great Horned Owl[2] | X | X | X | X |
| Elf Owl | X | X | X | X |
| White-Throated Swift | X | X | X | X |
| Black-Fronted Hummingbird | | | X | |
| Costa's Hummingbird | X | X | X | X |
| Xantus' Hummingbird[2] | | X | X | X |
| Gilded Flicker | X | X | X | X |
| Gray-Breasted Woodpecker | X | X | X | X |
| Ladder-Backed Woodpecker | X | X | X | X |
| Gila Woodpecker | X | X | X | X |
| Ash-Throated Flycatcher | X | X | X | X |

| CLASS AND BIRD NAME | Spring | Summer | Fall | Winter |
|---|---|---|---|---|
| Black Phoebe[2] | X | X | X | X |
| Say's Phoebe | | | X | X |
| Thick-Billed Kingbird | | X | | |
| Vermilion Flycatcher[3] | X | X | X | X |
| Tree Swallow | | | | X |
| Violet-Green Swallow | X | X | X | X |
| Common Raven | X | X | X | X |
| Western Scrub Jay | X | X | X | X |
| Verdin | X | X | X | X |
| Cactus Wren | X | X | X | X |
| Canon Wren[2] | X | X | X | X |
| Gray Thrasher | | X | | |
| Northern Mockingbird | X | X | X | X |
| Black-Tailed Gnatcatcher | X | X | X | X |
| Blue-Gray Gnatcatcher | X? | X? | X | X |
| California Gnatcatcher | X | X | X | X |
| White-Lored Gnatcatcher? | | X | | |
| Phainopepla | X | X | X | X |
| Loggerhead Shrike | X | X | X | X |
| Hooded Oriole | X | X | X | X |
| Cardinal | | X | | |
| Pyrrhuloxia | X | X | X | X |
| Black-Throated Sparrow | X | X | X | X |
| House Finch | X | X | X | X |
| Lark Sparrow | | | X | X |
| House Sparrow | X | X | X | X |
| White-Crowned Sparrow | | | X | X |
| Black-Throated Gray Warbler | | | X | X |
| Orange-Crowned Warbler | | | X | X |
| Wilson's Warbler | X | | X | X |

[1]Seen mainly at sea
[2]Seen in Mesquite Canyon
[3]Seen near golf course at Nopoló

We thank the generous folks at Danzante Eco-Resort for
letting us include this bird checklist.

10

LAND ACTIVITIES

El Campeón Panchito Reyes in action.

**11**

# Other Activities

- Boxing
- Community Involvement
- Cooking
- Off-Road Racing
- Painting
- Pilates
- Pool and Darts

# BOXING

Once a month, Loreto transforms from a peaceful, quiet fishing village into a vibrant center for Mexican boxing competition. Matches are held in the gymnasium, where a boxing ring is set up and sponsored by world boxing federations. Most of the town gathers to drink some beer and cheer on fighters from all over the Baja peninsula as they take on local Loreto fighters. While the fans are passionate, they are very supportive of all the fighters; there is never any booing, and the atmosphere is not raucous in the least. It is a fascinating family and community event and is an extremely valuable glimpse into Loreto culture.

Signs will be up around town in the weeks before the fights with the dates and times of the event. If you cannot find any signs, stop by the gym (on Francisco I. Madero) to inquire, or just ask a Loretano on the street; they will probably know. The Loretanos also have advertising cars that drive through the town with loudspeakers on top announcing significant town events, including boxing matches. Tickets can be purchased on the night of the event, with bleacher seats for $10 and floor seats for $20.

# COMMUNITY INVOLVEMENT

## Hidden Harbor Yacht Club

A love of the sea and sharing friendships and social activities has always been the heart of the Hidden Harbor Yacht Club (HHYC). The purpose of the club is to help friends and neighbors and to educate children. During the last twelve years, it has raised money to help send children to school, donated medical supplies to the local hospital, helped the cultural center, donated air-conditioners to the school for the handicapped, aided the **Internado School in Loreto** and **Ligui Dormitory** (Loreto College), provided the **Green Angels** with radios for roadside help, helped the bicycle club of Loreto, given financial aid to the battered mothers and children program in Loreto, given money to the alcohol treatment centers in town, and helped cruisers when they have had disasters.

Becoming a member of HHYC, an international club, not only gives the satisfaction of helping others locally—members can also enjoy privileges and events at other HHYC clubs around the world. Children under age 18 are considered junior members. Membership is only $10 per year

## The Master and the Prodigy

*The Master:* The figurehead of Loreto boxing is the dignified and sagacious Chicho Valenzuela. Identifiable by his boyish smile, glass eye, and bouncy strut, this local legend can almost always be found in El Gimnasio, where he selflessly works all day training the local fighters and setting up boxing events.

A former professional boxer, Chicho rarely brings up his tremendous achievements, and is quick to blush when his students brag about the time he knocked Oscar de la Hoya down for the first time in his career in 1993 (see for yourself by searching for "First Oscar droppage" on *www. youtube.com*), or when they mention the Mexican super lightweight championship title he once held. Always carrying an approachable, friendly demeanor, Chicho will be seen giving the patented "Chicho Slap," a quick horizontal hand slap followed by a gentle knuckle to knuckle pound, to all well-wishers. If you see him around town, flash him a big smile and wait for the grin and a "chicho slap." Just be ready to exchange your wittiest remarks as he is a sucker for one-liners (in Spanish, of course).

*The Prodigy:* Weighing in at 114 pounds (52 kilos), Francisco "Panchito" Reyes, super flyweight boxing champion of the Hispanic world, is Loreto's hometown hero. Gentle outside the ring but menacing inside, Panchito works hard toward his goal of being recognized and respected internationally for his talents. He runs over 6 miles (10 km) and does over 800 sit-ups every day. He carries himself with considerable grace. He is humble, soft-spoken, and it is always an honor to be in his laughing presence. Notwithstanding his mild manner, Panchito transforms into a ferocious fighter in the ring, capable of unleashing speedy combinations that land with pinpoint precision. If you happen to be in Loreto when a Panchito fight is the main event, you shouldn't miss it. El Campeón in action is Loreto's biggest sports attraction.

and the membership year runs from April 1 to March 31. There are currently 471 active members in the club.

*E-mail: Hiddenharboryachtclub@hotmail.com*

## Optimist Club

Though you already know that Loreto is full of hidden treasures, there is one that few people know about, but that does so many great things under the radar we felt compelled to mention it.

Established in 2004, the Optimist Club in Loreto is affiliated with **Optimist International**, an organization designed to help youth. Presently, this local chapter with seventy members is the biggest affiliate in Mexico.

The Loreto chapter certainly exemplifies the "Bringing out the best in kids" motto. Once a month, the club meets in the **Oasis Hotel** to discuss ways to help Loretano youth, and then during the month works to achieve those goals. The group is made up of residents old and new who all share a similar passion.

There are a variety of issues that the Optimists tackle. For example, they bought seventeen air-conditioners for the Loreto schools. They also donated computers to the local library and schools. The Optimists organize a number of fundraising events that double as community-building town events. There is an annual Pig Party, a pancake breakfast with Santa which the entire town attends, and a large **"Fishin' for the Mission"** event.

Each meeting entertains requests from locals. Recently a school-teacher came asking for $300 in order to increase security in her kindergarten classroom. The Optimists immediately granted her the money. The Optimists are a great group of people who generously donate their time and resources to help the Loreto community. Well done, Optimists! Visit their website or talk to Augie at **Augie's Bar and Bait Shop** on the Malecón for more information.

*Web: www.optimist.org*

## Loreto Bay Foundation

In 2006, the Loreto Bay Foundation announced the recipients of its inaugural grants. Eleven charities affiliated with Loreto were awarded grants totaling $64,350 to assist them in their efforts towards creating a better community. Among these are grants for animal welfare, health services, education, job creation, economic development, urban planning and environmental awareness. **The Loreto Environmental Center**, **Animalandia**, **Loreto campus of the state university** (UABCS), the **Loreto Fire Department**, and the **Center of Ecotourism and Sustainable Development at Stanford University**, among others, have been awarded funds.

A **nonprofit** organization, the Loreto Bay Foundation was established by **Loreto Bay Company** to serve the economic and social needs of the historic town of Loreto. Loreto Bay has partnered with **Fonatur**, Mexico's tourism development agency, to develop **The Villages of Loreto Bay**, an authentic Mexican seaside community in Baja California Sur. In the early stages of its partnership, Loreto Bay Company pledged to donate 1% of home sales back to the community as a way to help foster economic and social growth in the Loreto area. With residential real estate sales exceeding $200 million, Loreto Bay Company has pledged more than $2 million to the Loreto Bay Foundation to support local projects in education, extracurricular activities, business development, medical services, environmental protection and affordable housing. With bylaws aimed at conserving Loreto's natural beauty and protecting the nearby national marine park, the Loreto Bay Foundation's principles are aligned with the development of The Villages of Loreto Bay. Development practices include programs for sustainable energy, water renewal and land stewardship, as well as creating economic opportunities through new jobs and local businesses. For more foundation information, visit www.loretobayfoundation.org. (Author's note: 1% of the gross sales of *Best Guide: Loreto* is contributed to the Loreto Bay Foundation as well.)

# COOKING

### C&C Tours and Ground Services: Ceviche/Tortilla Cooking Class

C&C Tours invented a one-of-a-kind, instant-classic tourist activity: an instructional class on how to make ceviche, (raw seafood, marinated or "cooked" in a citrus mixture—a traditional seafood favorite) and tasty tortillas. For $35 per person you will get two classes (on the same day), in a kitchen where you will learn about and then execute the recipes yourself. For lunch you get to eat your own concoction, and when you depart, your chef instructors leave you a note card with the recipes so you can make them at home, too. All equipment and ingredients are included. A minimum of four people are required. C&C obviously knows how to satisfy tourists in unconventional ways.

*Location: Misión de San Ignacio, Nopoló*

# OFF-ROAD RACING

Off-road racing is big in Baja California, and Loreto doesn't miss out on the action. There is a cadre of racers in the area, including fifteen-time **Baja 1000 winner John Johnson**, who resides in **Juncalito**. In general, the racing community is considered a fraternity of drivers and fanatics who share their knowledge and stories by word of mouth. Pay attention to the signs and painted walls about local happenings in town—they stay current and keep you informed of off-road races (and other "underground" events, like horse races and cockfights).

## Baja 1000

This race from **Ensenada** to **La Paz** has been running every other year for over thirty-five years. It is held and organized by **SCORE International**, sponsored by Tecate beer, and opened to a wide variety of vehicle classes, such as modified cars and trucks, motorcycles, dune buggies, and ATVs. The Baja 1000 does not pass through Loreto, but if you drive into the mountains you can catch the action. The race is usually held in November. SCORE also hosts other off-road races such as the **Baja 500** in **Ensenada** as part of their popular desert series. Visit their website for dates, maps, and all the pertinent information.

*Web: www.score-international.com*

## Loreto 400

The Loreto 400 starts at the baseball stadium in Loreto. From there, the drivers cross the Baja peninsula to the Pacific side, and return back to Loreto on the same day. Drivers come from all around the state with all sorts of vehicles for this race, and the start draws packed crowds and makes for some quality entertainment. One year, a driver tried to show off and went flying out of the stadium, rolling his car and ruining his chances of winning only seconds after the opening gun. The race is usually held in mid-September around the time of the **Mexican day of independence, September 16**. Cash and trophies are awarded as prizes.

# PAINTING

### Weekly Painting Classes at Loreto Playa Bed and Breakfast

A week in Loreto would simply not be complete without spending a tranquil Monday morning at **Paulette Gochie's** Loreto Playa B&B learning to paint with the best of them. Paulette happily hosts the classes in her spacious garage, utilizing her expertise and local network to bring artists from America, Canada, and all over Mexico to teach the weekly sessions. Canadian transplant **Donna Dickson** (see **Galería Loreto**) instructed our course and shared her wisdom on the complexity of the watercolor medium. Prices run around $20 for a class featuring a guest artist or $8 for standard instruction, and all necessary materials are included if you know to ask for them in advance. The hands-on lesson will give you a better sense of the technical and compositional elements of painting, and after three hours you are likely to emerge with a work worthy of framing.

*Location: North Loreto on Calle Davis*
*Hours: 9:00 a.m. Sept.–May (Mon. Only)*
*Phone: 613-135-1129*
*Web: www.loretoplaya.com*

# PILATES

**Silvia Jañez** conducts pilates classes on the beach in front of the **Oasis Hotel** Monday through Thursday evenings at 7:00 p.m.

*Phone: 613-109-8995*

# POOL AND DARTS

One block north of **Cuatro Altos**, the primary pool hall in Loreto has five tables, rentable for $1.50 per hour. Chips and soft drinks are available. The tables are in pretty good shape.

Every Wednesday at 2:00 p.m., the **Hotel Oasis bar** hosts a quality dart competition. Call 613-135-1129 for more information, or just show up.

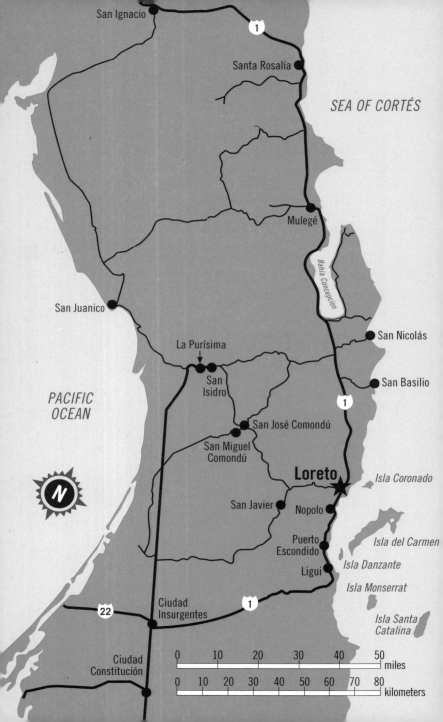

San Ignacio

1

Santa Rosalía

SEA OF CORTÉS

Mulegé

Bahía Concepción

San Juanico

La Purísima

San Isidro

San Nicolás

San Basilio

1

PACIFIC
OCEAN

San José Comondú

San Miguel
Comondú

**Loreto**

Isla Coronado

San Javier

Nopolo

Puerto
Escondido

Isla del Carmen

Isla Danzante

Ligui

Isla Monserrat

N

22

Ciudad
Insurgentes

1

Isla Santa
Catalina

Ciudad
Constitución

0    10    20    30    40    50
                                    miles

0   10  20  30  40  50  60  70  80
                                    kilometers

# South of Loreto

- El Juncalito Beach
- Puerto Escondido
- Tabor Canyon Hike
- Ligui/Ensenada Blanca
- Primer Agua
- Agua Verde
- San Javier
- The Loop Trip (San Juanico,
  La Purísima/San Isidro, Comondú)

If you're feeling adventurous, stir crazy, or both, take a day to drive south from Loreto to explore some of the less-developed neighboring areas. There is not much to do, but plenty of natural beauty makes a great setting for those who know how to make their own fun. Sailing, hiking, snorkeling, and eco-friendly adventurers will surely find their niche on the rocky **El Juncalito Beach**, the pristinely blue waters of **Puerto Escondido**, or the alternative resorts in the sandy hills of **Ensenada Blanca**.

Driving south from Loreto on Highway 1, there are two places that we feel should not be missed. If you are on the road around lunchtime, don't forget to stop and eat at **Vista del Mar**, an unassuming lone structure on the east side of the road only a five-minute drive from **Nopoló**. A secret among locals, Vista del Mar is authentically "Baja" in every way, which especially means great seafood. The chocolate clams are the house specialty and are sure to make you want to come back for more.

A bit farther south, the road twists and turns before finally opening onto an expansive view of the ocean. At Km 96 the shoulder widens at a prime lookout point. Here both tourists and locals pull their cars over to get out and gawk or take photos of the breathtaking view of the Sea of Cortés and nearby **Isla del Carmen** and **Isla Danzante**.

## EL JUNCALITO BEACH

At approximately Km 97+, a sign on the side of Highway 1 indicates that you have reached the head of the dirt road leading to El Juncalito, a sleepy palmed cove and beach community of RVs and modest residences along the water. There is a quiet, rocky beach that makes for a pleasant walk, and locals will kindly direct you to a panga owner who will take you fishing or on a trip to the surrounding islands for a reasonable fee.

For more private access to the beach, follow Highway 1 only a few hundred meters south of the El Juncalito turnoff, and continue down the bumpy dirt road until you reach the water. This is another nice place to relax, save for a fair share of litter left by previous careless visitors.

Our recommendation is to bring some snorkeling gear and venture into the hills for a short and relatively easy hike beginning at the south end of the beach. Only a half mile long, the hike leads over a hilltop where hikers can see at once both El Juncalito and the Sea of Cortés to the north, and the placid Puerto Escondido to the south. As the trail descends, hikers can choose to snorkel in a protected cove off the Sea of Cortés, or in the warm blue waters at the north end of **Puerto Escondido** where snorkeling isn't quite as good but the water is much calmer.

## PUERTO ESCONDIDO

Continuing farther south on Highway 1, you will reach the road to Puerto Escondido at Km 94. Apart from a single R.V. park (**Tripui RV Park & Hotel**), the dilapidated infrastructure that exists around this harbor is the vestige of Mexican tourism agency Fonatur's abandoned attempt to modernize the area's tourist facilities. There are wide, paved

Protected harbor of Puerto Escondido

boulevards; lamp posts; and city blocks—but no community. Apart from this, visitors will find a boat ramp, a dock, and a small futuristic looking Fonatur office and a misplaced, ill-conceived power station. Attempts at new construction have also recently begun along the water. Puerto Escondido opened a fuel dock in March 2006. Diesel fuel is being sold for the same price as you would pay at the PEMEX station in Loreto plus 10%. The hours for fueling are 8:00 a.m. to 5:00 p.m. Credit cards and checks are not accepted at this time but will be in the future.

Puerto Escondido is the best all-weather anchorage for larger boats in the Sea of Cortés. It is completely surrounded by land except for its 65-foot wide, 10-foot deep channel entrance. The outer harbor, known as the "Waiting Room," is also a good anchorage.

For landlubbers, the natural beauty of the harbor itself is the only true draw of the area. Whereas our well-intentioned picnic lunch on the dock left much to be desired, a later catamaran trip to **Honeymoon Cove** at **Isla Danzante** proved to be one of our most memorable days in the area. Check out www.BajaSail.net for more information on the different tour packages available. Bottom line: unless you have plans to hoist the sails and set out to sea, there isn't much to do here. As it stands, this beautiful natural port is rough around the edges.

Every May, the Hidden Harbor Yacht Club hosts "**Loreto Fest**" which has evolved into a music and art festival of local and cruising talent (www.hiddenharboryachtclub.com). Loreto Fest started with a bay clean up and has grown to a four-day event. The main event of Loreto Fest is still the clean up of the bay and surrounding area. Events include a ham radio test, games, a regatta, a dinghy-kayak parade, beading classes, a watercolor workshop, jam sessions, a music harmony workshop, a basic guitar workshop and nautical-themed seminars.

## Tripui R.V. Park & Hotel

Halfway between the **Puerto Escondido** turn off and the blue waters of Puerto Escondido's central harbor sits Tripui R.V. Park and Hotel, the best choice for local accommodations and basic services, if only for lack of other options. The expansive, grassy layout is an appealing transition from the concrete and desert that otherwise comprise this area. Stop here for lunch or dinner in the on-site restaurant/bar, wash your clothes in their laundromat facility, pick up a snack in the adjoining minimart, or check your email in the modest Internet café. The R.V. park offers 133 permanent spaces and 21 overnight spaces. The hotel is made up of six air-conditioned rooms. A large swimming pool also adds to the draw. If you are on the road in an R.V. and want to stop over in Puerto Escondido, this, by default, is your place. Cash only.

*Location: Fifteen miles south of Loreto*
*Phone: 613-133-0814*
*E-mail: tripuivacation@hotmail.com*
*Web: www.tripui.com*

## TABOR CANYON HIKE

Opposite the turnoff to **Puerto Escondido**, a dirt road runs west into the mountains to the base of Tabor Canyon. Average-Joe hikers beware: even if you have the physical endurance to boulder-hop and trail blaze your way to the top of this ninety-minute hike, the hardest part is finding the trail to get you there. Most importantly, about twenty minutes into the hike, the solution to advancing involves maneuvering *under* two large boulders that block the arroyo. Our suggestion: hire a guide or someone who knows the area to take you. This will save you a considerable amount of time and energy that can otherwise be invested in reaching the top of the strenuous climb, where a beautiful waterfall and oasis await your arrival.

## LIGUI/ENSENADA BLANCA

A 10-minute drive past **Puerto Escondido** are Ligui and Ensenada Blanca. The town of Ligui is an unimpressive, run-of-the-mill Baja town. Driving along the maze of dirt roads here, it's hard to believe that any tourist would seek this place as a destination. Nevertheless, **The Villa Group**, located in Cabo San Lucas, has successfully completed the purchase of a huge oceanfront parcel on the bay and is now in the design and construction phase of a large destination resort.

To enter Ligui, turn east down a dirt road around Km 84. To get to Ensenada Blanca and the two eco-resorts hidden deep in the surrounding desert, take a right at the first fork in the road. The dirt road continues on for quite a while, and eventually you will come to a body of water, which is the northern end of Ensenada Blanca and the site of a local fishing camp. Follow the road as it forks right once again, and about five to ten minutes later you will pass a modestly marked turnoff for **El Santuario Eco-Retreat Center**. If you follow the road in the general direction of an impressive building perched on a raised peak ahead of you, you will arrive at the unmarked base of the elusive **Danzante Adventure Resort**.

## El Santuario Eco-Retreat Center

When they say eco-retreat, they mean it. This place is committed to its green aims. Organically rustic and wholesome, El Santuario offers seven modest yet comfortable bungalows called *casitas*, with a two-story lofted option for larger groups or families. The smaller casitas are offered at a rate of $85 per night for single occupancy or $66 per person per night for double occupancy ($132 per night). A large central yurt is used as a yoga and meditation room, and three meals a day are served in an open-air casita which functions as the resort's kitchen. The facility offers four gravity showers—you fill your own overhead tank with a predetermined amount of shower water, then open the spout to release the water in a small spray. All toilets are dry and compost based. In addition to the yoga/meditation sessions, El Santuario offers hikes, kayaking trips, and boats out to the surrounding islands. If you are a fan of this truly eco-friendly approach to vacationing and don't mind sparing a few luxuries to do so, this is a lovely place to relax for a few days.

*Phone: 805-541-7921 (in USA); 613-104-4254*

*E-mail: baja@el-santuario.com*

*Web: www.el-santuario.com*

## Danzante Adventure Resort

Whereas the nearby El Santuario is an eco-resort in the most organic sense, Danzante Adventure Resort offers a more luxurious, all-inclusive eco-option, with a price tag to match. The resort was built from all-natural materials, runs on 100% solar power, and pledges to employ only locals. Nine clean, comfortable suites sit at the crest of the resort's hilltop perch, each with a terrace for taking in the magnificent view of the Sea of Cortés. All standard, unguided activities, as well as three health-conscious meals per day, are included in the rate. Optional activities for

A view from the deck of Danzante Eco-Resort

an additional charge include guided kayaking, scuba diving, fishing, horseback riding, island exploring, and whale-watching trips. Danzante is the ultimate escape for those with the time and money to afford it. Rates average $400 per night and you need reservations.

*Phone: 408-354-0042 (in USA)*

*Web: www.danzante.com*

## PRIMER AGUA

Many tour outfitters offer trips to the oasis Primer Agua via hiking, bike, ATV, or horseback. However you choose to go, you may want to stop by the Fonatur office in **Nopoló**, 613-133-0245, to obtain a permit to enter for $10 per person (even though no one will be waiting at the oasis to check—it's better to be safe). The not-completely-graded dirt road is 5 miles (8 km) long and begins at Km 114 on Highway 1. With picnic tables and a swimming area, Primer Agua used to be a popular weekend vacation destination for the locals until the new permitting requirements made it more difficult and more expensive. Now, mostly tourists go to observe birds and wildlife of all sorts congregating for a drink. Where there is water, there is life, which is why the lush oasis has been occupied and appreciated for thousands of years. Winter is the best time to visit, and the closer to summer you get, the more arid the terrain will be, with less green and fewer animals. On a return visit in late July, it was dry.

Primer Agua—the "first water" found in the Baja Peninsula.          Photo by Sara Axelrod

### C&C Tours and Ground Services: Primer Agua Group Trip

For large groups of at least twenty people, C&C offers trips to Primer Agua oasis. Included in the $100-per-person fee is an all-you-can-eat fish, clam, and chicken barbeque, with unlimited alcohol. Blankets are provided so you can enjoy a picnic-style meal if you choose to. The entry fee via Fonatur (Mexican tourism bureau) is covered, so you and your party don't have to worry about anything. The more people in your group, the lower the price per person.

## AGUA VERDE

After Highway 1 bends southwest away from the coast, look for the turnoff to Bahía Agua Verde between Km 63 and 64. You'll be holding your breath and praying there's no oncoming traffic as you navigate the switchbacks on the bumpy, winding 25-mile-long (41-km) dirt road, recommended for four-wheel drive, high-clearance vehicles (only!); the road is not passable for trailers.

Agua Verde is perfect for the type of person who loves to set up a tent on the beach and can make a grand adventure out of next to nothing.

Don't go and expect to have any fun activities waiting for you other than lying in the sand. While the scenery is beautiful, the hamlet—if you'd even call it that—at the end of road is unsightly and unaccommodating. If there's any prize for enduring the drive and reaching the final destination, it is Agua Verde's cove, a great boater's choice for anchoring, which features a stunning little sandbar beach. We consider Agua Verde a day trip because of its proximity to Loreto, but in actuality, only solitude-seeking campers who stay overnight will find it a worthwhile trip. The entire ride from Loreto to the end of the road takes two to three hours.

## SAN JAVIER

The road to San Javier begins at Km 118, off Highway 1 only a short distance south of downtown Loreto. The dirt road (very bumpy) is in the process of being paved up to **Rancho Las Parras** about 12 miles (19 km) in. Whatever piece of road remains unpaved when you read this, be prepared for a bumpy ride. Approximately 10 miles (16 km) in, you'll be on the original mission trail, leading you around sharp turns and jagged cliffs through the Sierra la Giganta. The road is definitely not recommended for the inexperienced driver. Crosses scattered along the road and fallen cars visible in the valley below serve as reminders of how dangerous the trip can be. Think twice about taking your rental car up. Instead, make the drive with a reliable tour company. If you do choose to drive yourself, make sure you do so in a high-clearance, preferably four-wheel-drive vehicle, and give a soft beep as you approach dramatic curves to warn any potential oncoming traffic. The whole drive is about 22 miles (36 km) long, and takes almost two hours to complete. It is hard to imagine **Padre Francisco María Piccolo** and his ten trusted soldiers carving a road out of this rugged terrain in 1699 (it took them twelve days). The labors of these intrepid men were the beginning of the expansion of the missionary system in the Californias.

On the way, you will pass faded and relatively unimpressive cave paintings, as well as the historic **Rancho Las Parras**, one of the oldest ranches in the Californias. On their journey to establish a route to San Javier, **Padre Piccolo** and his men came upon this large patch of wild grapes and named it, appropriately, "Grapevine Ranch." Some history

San Javier Mission                                    Photo by David Axelrod

suggests that the oldest structures at Rancho Las Parras date back to 1757. The ranch was founded by two Spaniards who came to San Javier to help with the construction of the church. For over 150 years, the ranch was owned by the **de los Santos family**, descendents of a Portuguese sailor who jumped ship around 1850 and ended up marrying into the family which owned the property. All the owners throughout the centuries have maintained the olive, mango, and orange orchards planted by these earliest owners. We bought an entire crate of mangoes for thirty pesos on our way to San Javier.

At Km 16+ you will pass the site of **Rancho Viejo**, the actual first site of the San Javier mission founded by Padre Piccolo in 1699. In 1707, the site of the present village was developed, and in 1720, the mission was moved here. In 1744, **Padre Miguel del Barco** started construction on the beautiful stone church that stands today, well-preserved. It is built from basalt stone blocks quarried nearby. Due to a lack of master builders to guide the native workers, the church took fourteen years to build and was completed in 1758.

The church is in excellent condition with original walls, floors, windows, and religious artifacts. It is still in use, usually open every day from 7:00 a.m. to 6:00 p.m. Mass is said every second Wednesday of the month by a visiting priest from Loreto. On December 2 and 3 of each year, the small agricultural village of about 150 fills with people from all over the area to celebrate the birthday of the village's namesake.

San Javier was California's second mission, situated in the fertile **Viggé-Biaundó** valley. Today, San Javier is a charming town with one cobblestone street leading up to the mission. Adobe and thatched-roof homes keep locals cool in the intense heat, and while there is electricity, it is only turned on for three hours a day in the morning.

There is only one restaurant in the town, **Restaurante Palapa San Javier**, open for lunch and dinner, which offers simple meals and cold beverages.

The ornate mission sits in front of a scenic mountain backdrop. However, there are other attractions. In the orchards behind the church, a 300-year-old olive tree rests in the shade. Citrus, grapes, figs, and, most notably, onions, irrigated by canals built by the earliest Jesuits, also grow here. Sugar lovers should be sure to taste some of the region's specialty sweets—the rich marmalade candy is a worthwhile addition to the ride home.

If you need a place to stay for the night, your best bet is **Casa Doña Ana**, where cabañas, each with a private bathroom, are available for approximately $35 per person per night.

**C&C Tours and Ground Services** offers day trips for $120 per person, with a six-person minimum. Fruit and breakfast in the insured, eight-passenger van as well as lunch in the town are included. You will stop at Rancho Las Parras and a goat ranch farther down the road.

**Cormorant Dive Center** charges $119 each with a two-person minimum. If you go to San Javier with Cormorant, ask for Juve to take you there—he's a great guy with tons of expertise, and you'll ride in an air-conditioned sport utility vehicle. Mountain biking and ATV trips are also available to San Javier through Cormorant.

A view of the winding road to San Javier

Photo by Sara Axelrod

# THE LOOP TRIP (SAN JUANICO, LA PURÍSIMA/SAN ISIDRO, COMONDÚ)

Looking at a map, you may think that the fastest way to get to La Purísima and Comondú from Loreto would be either to head straight west toward San Javier, or to drive north on Highway 1 and then turn inland just before the southern end of Bahía Concepción. But those two routes would force you to drive on the slowest, bumpiest dirt roads, and neither is the easiest route to make the adventurous northwest/inland road trip out of Loreto. The best way to go is to drive south out of Loreto on Highway 1 to **Ciudad Insurgentes**, then head north on the paved but potholed Highway 53. Distance-wise, it's much longer, but trust us, it's much faster. You would be wise to take the northwestward detour to the surf mecca of San Juanico on the Pacific Coast before doubling back to La Purísima. If you choose to proceed to Comondú, complete the loop back to Highway 53 and south to Ciudad Insurgentes the way you came. Or, when you are heading east out of San Isidro and the road splits to either Comondú or northeast back to the sea, choose the latter option by staying left at the fork, leading you back to the eastern coast and to the phenomenal beaches of Bahía Concepción.

## *San Juanico*

Tucked away in a remote region of western Baja California Sur, San Juanico has survived over the years as a small fishing village, isolated from the rest of the world and accessible even now only by narrow dirt roads. However, the discovery of what many consider to be the best surfing in the Baja region has turned it into a hot spot for surf culture.

The twenty-mile (32-km) beachfront, stretching from the mouth of the **San Gregorio River** to the end of **Punta Pequeña**, has six separate breaks, each of them offering slightly different surfing conditions. The breaks (simply named Points One through Six) are named in numerical order starting from town. They are all spectacular right breaks, formed by volcanic rock and sandbars gradually sloping into the sea. First Point is the gentlest and great for learning, while Second Point is the most consistent and popular break.

However, Third Point is where the greatest waves occur. The southern swell gets picked up by the submerged sand bar and can cause perfect overhead waves with rides of well over 330 feet (100 m). Points Four through Six are not nearly as well documented and are considered the secret breaks for the locals. Rumor has it that occasionally waves will link up between Fourth Point and First Point around the month of September, causing picturesque double-overhead waves that offer a once-in-a-lifetime ride.

Food and accommodations are very simple in San Juanico. An American couple recently moved in and created a fabulous set of campgrounds, palapas, and guesthouses along with an all-day restaurant and Internet access. You can't miss it, as these are the only accommodations in **Scorpion Bay Park** (just on the edge of San Juanico; phone: 613-138-2850, www.scorpionbay.net), and the park is generally packed with surfers. Campsites are $7 per night; palapas with showers are $36 per night for two people, and $60 per night for four people; and four-person guesthouses are $125 per night. Internet access is expensive, and is roughly $9 per hour.

Dining options are very limited. The best place to eat is the **Cantina**, which is part of the Scorpion Bay complex. It is open from 8:00 a.m. to 10:00 p.m. every day, and has very clean kitchens that serve a wide range of breakfast, lunch, and dinner entrees. It is very reasonably priced, the food is tasty, and the portion sizes are good. **Alacrán's Pizza** is located between Scorpion Bay and San Juanico central, and a number of taco stands and hole-in-the-wall restaurants round out the dining options.

## La Purísima and San Isidro

The twin cities of La Purísima and San Isidro sit on the doorstep of the majestic **Cerro El Pilón**, a jagged desert rock spire in an oasis of lush palm trees and vegetation. While the scenery is breathtaking, the towns themselves are far from noteworthy, except for their historical significance as mission sites. The recreational tourist will find himself heartbroken when he shows up in town and tries to find a nice place to spend the night, get some food, or even pass ten minutes while a member of the party looks for a toilet. San Isidro and La Purísima are towns that exist only as workstations to take advantage of the only arable land within hundreds of square miles, and are not well established for tourism. The only real attraction is the ruin that was once **Misión La Purísima Concepción**, founded by **Padre Nicolás Tamaral** in 1717. Accommodations and food are hard to come by. **Motel Nelva** is the only place where you can consistently find lodging; it is located next-door to the police station, so while it is very plain, it is also very safe. Simple rooms with shared showers and bathrooms are available for $15 per night. If you ask around, it is also possible to find some guesthouses in the area, but they are rarely open. The only restaurant is the elusive **Abarrotes Neferik**, which locals seem to have conspired to keep hidden by always pointing gringos in the wrong direction.

La Purísima and San Isidro are located in a geographically unique and spectacular area well worth seeing. This is an ideal place to visit if you are in search of a fabulous place to go backpacking into the wilderness or want to gaze at the emblematic Cerro El Pilón. But, it is definitely not recommended for anything other than ecotourism. It is a sufficient place to re-supply, as it has a medical clinic, grocery store, barrels of gas for sale, and other necessities.

## Comondú

Southwest of San Isidro, Comondú can only be accessed by the kind of road that you'd rather not drive on—rocky, winding, and definitely recommended only for high-clearance vehicles. Make sure you stay right (continuing straight) when the road splits just over 2 miles (3 km) east out of San Isidro. The road descends steeply into the 7-mile-long (11-km) arroyo entering Comondú, which is a general name for two neighboring towns, **San José de Comondú** and **San Miguel de Comondú**. The picturesque valley makes both towns ideal for growing crops of date palms, figs, sugarcane, mangoes, and more.

The original **San José de Comondú** mission, founded in 1708, was located north of present-day San José de Comondú in Comondú. The deteriorated site is presently being restored, though any sign of progress is unnoticeable. In 1737, the mission moved south to San José, but was later torn down and replaced by a school. Now all that remains is an old residence once used for missionaries, now used as a church.

Two miles (3 km) west is San Miguel de Comondú, which is on the way back southwest toward Ciudad Insurgentes. San Miguel has a small restaurant and very basic shop.

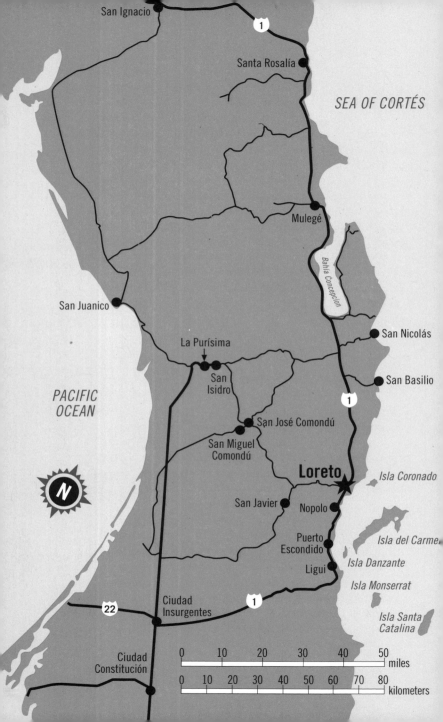

# North of Loreto

- Bahía Concepción
- Mulegé
- Santa Rosalía

# BAHÍA CONCEPCIÓN

Bahía Concepción, which begins just 60 miles (96 km) north of Loreto and immediately south of **Mulegé**, is lined with over fifty miles of truly gorgeous beaches, one after the other. Highway 1 follows along the coast, providing easy access to them all. There are also small islands scattered throughout the bay, making it ideal for sailors and kayakers. The views are breathtaking and the drive is really a thrill.

On the way up to Bahía Concepción, at Km 62 (counting from Loreto, northbound), there is a small dirt road leading to the small fishing villages of **San Nicolás** and **San Sebastián**. At Km 60, a left turn will take you up to **San Isidro** and **La Purísima**.

The most noteworthy of the beaches along Bahía Concepción are Playa El Requesón, Playa El Burro, Playa Coyote, and Playa Santispec.

### Playa El Requesón

At Km 92+ you'll find this spectacular sandbar beach that connects the mainland to a small island (**Isla Requesón**) only a short distance away. You won't want to leave, so park your car on the beach or set up a tent and camp for the night. Also, from the beach there is a great view of a spectacular petrograph, perched on the mountainside.

Photo by Alan Axelrod

### Playa Buenaventura

Traveling north you will come across this beach at Km 95, home to **Hotel Buenaventura** (rooms $60 to $100, phone 615-153-0408) and **George's Ole Sports Bar and Grill** (8:00 a.m. to 10:00 p.m.).

### Playa El Coyote

Continuing along to Km 108 you'll find an R.V. park near this beach (which is usually quite crowded and for good reason), and **Playa El Burro** at Km 109, with beach palapas, bathroom facilities, and Bertha's Restaurant—making it a great pick for camping out. **EcoMundo—Baja Tropicales** is just north of El Burro. It is an extremely environment-friendly eco-resort that provides accommodations ($12 for a standard palapa, $6 for camping), showers, and a restaurant. Kayaks can be rented for $25 to $50, depending on your level of experience and how long you're out. Snorkeling equipment is available, too.

### Playa Santispec

Finally, at Km 114, is this trailer-friendly beach—so much so that all the spots are taken and tend to be occupied year round. It is the northern-most beach on Bahía Concepción, and is quite popular.

About 15 miles (24 km) south of Mulegé, the **Aman Hotel** chain is purportedly building one of their exquisite six-star resorts on a private bay.

# MULEGÉ

Huddled around the **Mulegé River**, just 38 miles (61 km) south of **Santa Rosalía**, sits a small but attractive little town, Mulegé. An oasis of lush date palms in the middle of dry, barren Baja, Mulegé is a perfect side trip for those in search of prime hiking, diving, or simply looking for a quiet and remote place to relax. Unlike Santa Rosalía, a very authentic Baja town, Mulegé's population of 5,000 supports itself primarily on tourism. If only for this reason, the residents are friendly and helpful, very willing to direct you to the beach, the mission, or the local bar. Downtown Mulegé is quite small, but shops, restaurants, and bars abound near the main square.

On the hill opposite the oasis, you will find the **Misión Santa Rosalía de Mulegé**, which has served the town since the early 1700s. Inside stands the original statue of the town's patron saint, a relic of Mulegé's three-century-long history and its continued relevance to the community today. Perhaps the most impressive feature is its lookout, only a short hike behind the mission's hilltop perch. From this vantage point, you get an incredible view of the oasis below—a perfect photo-op, especially at sunset.

The historic museum, also known as the "Old Prison Museum," provides another hilltop viewpoint on the north side of town. The prison was known as the "prison without locks," as inmates were allowed to hold jobs in town under the condition that they would return each evening when the prison's horn sounded at 6:00 p.m. The prison was in operation until the mid-1970s, and about 20 years ago the space was converted into a museum.

Photo by Sara Axelrod

Misión Santa Rosalía de Mulegé

Those in search of another killer view and/or a feel for Mulegé's (albeit uneventful) history will enjoy a peek into the prison cells, a detailed explanation of its operation, and a miscellaneous assortment of artifacts. At the end of Calle Cananea, Mon.–Fri. 9:00 a.m.–1:00 p.m., donations requested.

While some of the most beautiful beaches in the area, and the best snorkeling spots, can be found 16 miles (26 km) south on the breathtaking **Bahía Concepción**, Mulegé's **Playa Punta Prieta** is a serene spot closer to town. Right where the Mulegé River meets the Sea of Cortés, this large, empty expanse of sandy beach has river and sea views on either side. A blocked-off path leads uphill to the town's lighthouse, which curious travelers may find worthy of exploration. The beach also offers satisfactory snorkeling, particularly along the south end by the lighthouse.

Mulegé lighthouse

The crux of this town's claim to fame as a verdant oasis, the Mulegé River, runs inland from the Sea of Cortés and offers a host of possible activities to visitors. The **Mulegé River** is not actually a river; it is an *estuario* (estuary), a brackish arm off the Sea of Cortés. If you have a fishing pole, there are plenty of spots along the riverbank to fish for a couple of hours. The river is also a great place to kayak; kayaks can be rented from **EcoMundo** (*Km 111; 615-153-0320*), for $25 per day for a single and $35 per day for a double. EcoMundo also leads guided half-day or multi-day trips, which cost about $50 per person per day. The dirt roads that run the length of either side of the river also make for a great walk, jog, bicycle, or ATV ride.

## *Activities*

### Cave Paintings
The extensive Indian cave paintings are one of Mulegé's primary tourist attractions and were deemed by UNESCO to be **World Heritage Sites**. Due to this fact, the beautiful, mural-style paintings have been stringently protected by locals and may only be accessed with a licensed guide. There are two different popular cave painting sites, **Cañón La**

179

**Trinidad**, and **San Borjitas**, both of which require an entire day trip to reach. Cañón La Trinidad is the most well known of the cave painting destinations, and is located within the boundaries of Rancho La Trinidad, 18 miles (29 km) west of Mulegé. Be prepared for an adventurous hike through a narrow, rocky canyon. During the wetter season you may need to cross several streams along the way. Within the rocky caves there are numerous painting sites, with one standout image of the **"Trinidad Deer,"** considered to be one of the finest indigenous cave paintings on the peninsula. *San Borjitas,* another popular cave-art site, depicts an estimated sixty human figures in all colors and sizes, and can be accessed by foot or by mule. **Baja Adventure Tours/Ciro Cuesta Romero** is our recommendation for a licensed guide outfitter. They speak solid English and are very well versed in local knowledge and history.

*Location: Calle Madero across from the church in the heart of Mulegé*
*Phone: 615-153-0530*
*E-mail: cirocuesta@yahoo.com.mx*

## Diving and Snorkeling

Diving is one of the most popular activities in Mulegé, and key dive spots are the offshore islands **Isla San Marcos** and **Isla Santa Inés**, which provide an array of colorful sea life.

Green Sea Turtle

### Cortez Explorers

Cortez Explorers, run by English couple **Bea and Andy Sidler**, offers the most respectable service in town. They have a custom dive boat and well-maintained equipment, not to mention certified local guides and reasonable prices. Snorkel trips run for roughly $30 per person, guided dives anywhere from $50 to $90 per person, depending on whether or not you rent equipment.

*Location: Cortez Explorers at 75A Moctezuma*
*Phone: 615-153-0500*
*Web: www.cortez-explorers.com*

# Food & Drink

## Saturday Night "Carnitas" at La Serenidad
No matter where you are staying in Mulegé, if you are in town on a Saturday night, we recommend eating dinner at La Serenidad's weekly pig roast feast. It is not the most authentically Mexican option around, but it is a fun and entertaining evening and a longstanding tradition in the area.

## Taquería Doney
Mulegé has some of the best and cheapest street food in Baja California, and this taco stand is about as good as it gets. Right in the heart of town, Doney offers the standard list of beef, chicken, and fried-shrimp tacos with a host of different do-it-yourself toppings, for around $1 each. A great lunch spot if you are in town midday!

# Night Life
Mulegé is a very small town, and the few central streets become surprisingly congested with traffic at night. Cruising may be the primary local pastime come nightfall, but a stroll around the four or five blocks that comprise the area should lead you past some quieter bars that may strike your fancy. The two below are our recommendations for those of you looking for the bonafide "places to go" in Mulegé at night.

## El Candil
A favorite among American and Canadian transplants in the area, this bar is right around the corner from El Pelícano and offers tables perfect for people-watching in the heart of town.

## El Pelícano
Right in Mulegé's main square, El Pelícano is the place where local gringos go to relax and have some reasonably-priced drinks. A standard watering hole, this down-home Mexican pub should adequately quench your thirst.

# Accommodations

## Hotel Hacienda Mulegé

This eighteenth-century hacienda is a good option for travelers with smaller budgets. Centrally located in the heart of Mulegé, the **Hotel Hacienda** offers lovely Spanish-style courtyards, a small swimming pool, and twenty-one clean and comfortable rooms. The hotel is well known for its popular café and bar, which has satellite TV featuring sporting events and offers similarly low-priced meals. Cash only; $35/room. Free parking. Amenities include restaurant/bar, small swimming pool, laundry service, tourist guide services, and AC/TV in rooms.

*Location: Calle Francisco Madero No. 3*
*Phone: 615-153-0021*

## La Serenidad

Just a couple of minutes' drive south of central Mulegé at Km 3, La Serenidad is a mid-priced retreat that lives up to its name. The hotel has been operated by American **Don Johnson** and his family for more than thirty-five years. This certainly seems to be the place to stay for the gringos visiting the area, given its adjoining private airstrip, longevity, and relaxing atmosphere. For around $70 per night you can get a queen-size bed and a comfortable, air-conditioned room, plus access to the pool with swim-up bar. The scene is nice, but not overdone, and everything is well maintained. Expect typical hotel amenities, décor, and English-speaking guests. Larger casitas offer two bedrooms and two baths, a small living area, and a terrace; a perfect solution for larger groups. An adjacent R.V. park offers ten spaces with full hook-up. Probably the biggest draw is La Serenidad's famous Saturday night pig roasts. Each week, gringos from the surrounding areas make a point of attending the fiesta, which offers a delicious all-you-can-eat dinner for $15 and a mariachi band to accompany your meal. If you have plans to visit Mulegé, we recommend you do it on a Saturday night to get a piece of the action. Prices are $72 double, $89 one bedroom suite, $128 two-bedroom casitas. Mastercard and Visa accepted. Amenities include restaurant/bar, swimming pool with bar, and AC in rooms.

*Location: Off Highway 1 at 3 km south of central Mulegé*
*Phone: 615-153-0540*

*Web: www.serenidad.com*

## Orchard Vacation Village & RV Park

If you're looking to avoid the typical tourist destination and stay somewhere a little more local, be sure to visit Orchard. We recommend their beautiful, newly constructed, family-size tropical villas, which sleep three couples and offer full eight-hour maid and cook service, for $121 per day. This price also gives you access to Orchard's lagoon-style pool, recently completed in August 2006. The facility also continues to stay true to its R.V.-park roots, offering a daily hook-up rate of $15.95 (monthly rates are also available). A third and more reasonably priced option is a rustic bungalow for $38 per night, though they are not our recommended choice.

*Location: 1 mile south of Central Mulegé on Highway 1*
*Phone: 1-866-317-3221 (toll free from USA)*
*E-mail: orchardvvv@prodigy.net.mx*
*Web: www.orchardvacationvillage.com*

## Resort at Punta Chivato

This luxurious hotel is owned by the **Posada de Las Flores** group, which you may be familiar with due to their namesake hotel in the heart of Loreto. Punta Chivato offers the same top-notch accommodations as its Loretan relation, but is far more remote. Twenty-six miles (42 km) north of Mulegé, the hotel sits along the Sea of Cortés on the famously

gorgeous **Santa Inés Bay**. Standard rooms ($240 to $270) boast lovely garden views with terraces and swing chairs, and beachfront Junior suites ($320 to $350) offer pristine views of water and balconies with sun beds. A tour company operates from the hotel's main lobby and can coordinate any type of regional excursion. Activities include tennis, kayaking, boat rental, mountain biking, snorkeling, fishing, or hiking. Don't overlook the utter relaxation of sunbathing by the hotel pool or on the beach. All meals are included in the room price and children under age 12 are not allowed. Visa and Mastercard accepted. Amenities include two restaurants, bar, swimming pool, tennis court, tour desk, video library, Internet satellite desk, satellite TV in public areas, and in-room AC, TV/VCR, and minibar.

*Location: Twenty-six miles north of Mulegé in Punta Chivato*

*Phone: 615-153-0188*

*Web: www.posadadelasflores.com*

Our take: Mulegé is every bit the "oasis in the middle of the desert" that it claims to be. Though there is no argument that it is second to Loreto in both charm and natural beauty, it is certainly a fun getaway for those with the time and interest to venture outside of Loreto proper. Though many activities are offered here, all of them (with the exception of the cave paintings) are offered in Loreto as well. We recommend you go for the Carnitas feast and simply relax in the shade of the region's verdant palms.

## SANTA ROSALÍA

A French copper-mining company, **El Boleo** (named after the balls of copper ore mined from the surrounding hills), founded this quaint coastal town in the 1880s. Though the mines have been closed since 1954, this French influence and mining history can be seen in virtually every aspect of the town today.

If you are traveling to Mulegé and are looking for a taste of authentic Baja culture (with a French flair), Santa Rosalía should not be missed. Twenty-four hours is all you need to make the most of what this personable ex-mining town has to offer. Although the view of a decrepit stretch of beach and an uninviting "Welcome to Santa Rosalía" sign on the side of Highway 1 indicate that you have reached your destination, you will quickly find that the charm of the town and its people far out-strip its unattractiveness. Those who stop to peek into the Santa Rosalían life will find the town an enjoyable place if they know where to go and what to do.

## Food & Drink

### Ángel Café
Right in the heart of town on **Avenida Obregón**, Ángel Café is a good place to sit down for a meal. The food is good, the prices are low, and the women who work here are kind and attentive, though service is a bit slow. The shaded oútdoor patio is a great place to sit and get a glimpse of a day in the life of a Santa Rosalían.

### Hotel Francés Restaurant
The restaurant in this famous hotel is only open for breakfast, from 7:00 a.m. to noon and is, in our opinion, the best way to enjoy this historic landmark.

Rowboats in Santa Rosalía

## La Michoacana

Right across the street from the bakery (Panadería El Boleo), Michoacana sells virtually every type of fruit treat you can imagine. Fresh fruit juices and smoothies go well with a bakery treat, but the real gems are their delicious natural fruit popsicles. In more flavors than you could count on two hands, these popsicles are the perfect way to beat the Baja heat.

## Panadería El Boleo

In Santa Rosalía, this bakery is as old as it is famous. It has been around as long as the French mining company after which it was named. This is a perfect place to pick up a snack or a quick breakfast on the go. The baguettes are a well-known favorite but ask the cashier for her recommendations. This stop is guaranteed to yield some very tasty results. Located in the heart of town on **Avenida Obregón** and open daily.

# *Accommodations*

## Casitas Hotel and Bar

Built in 2002, this is the newest lodging facility in town, and it shows. Guests are given their own private casitas, nicely furnished, with an incredible balcony terrace overlooking the water. The owner is kind and very responsive to guests. Other facilities include a hotel bar and a hot tub. At $56 per night for a shared deck area and $61 for a personal terrace, this is the highest-quality facility we found. An additional bonus for peso-less travelers: Casitas is one of the few Mexican establishments with a correct price conversion into American dollars.

*Location: Off of Highway 1 less than a kilometer south of town*

## Hotel El Morro

A fairly dated accommodation, El Morro beckons travelers with a beautifully tended flower garden along the front of the building, and a long, cliffside terrace along the back, overlooking the water. Rooms run in the $40 to $45 range with sterile white bathrooms and sparse furnishings. The adjacent restaurant provides unimpressive food and is relatively pricey. We recommend you spend the extra $10 and drive a couple of minutes up the road to the **Casitas Hotel and Bar**.

One of Hotel Francés' wooden porches

### Hotel Francés

Founded in 1886, this historic French colonial-style building is virtually as old as the town itself. The small rooms have adjoining wooden porches in the back that overlook a small courtyard pool. While this may be one of the most historical places to stay, it has neither the seaside view nor the modernity of the newer options listed above. Indeed, its age shows: the creaky wooden floors make the Hotel Francés a bit spooky during the night. Our recommendation: stop by for breakfast at the hotel's well-known restaurant.

## *Activities*

### Iglesia Santa Barbara

The cultural and geographic heart of the town was designed by famous French architect **Alexandre Gustave Eiffel** in 1884. This church of stamped steel sheet squares and trusses was designed and built in Paris and then disassembled and shipped to Santa Rosalía. Don't let the name fool you. Although this is one of the most impressive buildings in town, it is no Eiffel tower. Its modest façade does not diminish its significance as the heart and soul of Santa Rosalían life, however. Masses are held every day at 7:00 p.m., and all throughout the morning and evening on Sundays. The daily masses generate an impressive attendance and are worth sitting in on if you are seeking a true feel for this community and a vibrant introduction to Spanish-style gospel music.

## Museum of Mining History

Located in Santa Rosalía's old city, up on the **Mesa Francesa**, this museum, the **Museo Histórico Minero de Santa Rosalía**, was the former headquarters of the **El Boleo Mining Company**. The interior was left intact with the original furnishings and accoutrements of its heyday. The museum has a good deal of historical mining equipment and tools, as well as other antiques of interest. It is certainly worth a visit for those travelers seeking a better sense of the town's mining history. Admission is $1.30.

*Hours: 8:00 a.m.–2:00 p.m. and 5:00 p.m.–7:00 p.m. (Mon.–Sat.)*

## The Malecón

Like Loreto, Santa Rosalía is home to a lovely waterfront walkway that provides premium views of the Sea of Cortés and the town itself. Lined with palm trees and white wrought-iron benches, a sunset stroll along the Malecón is a relaxing (and romantic) way to enjoy Santa Rosalía.

## Local Soccer Games

Just a short way inland from Santa Rosalía's main strip lies a large sports oval widely utilized by the locals for community soccer matches. Such matches take place between teams of all ages and levels of experience and are well attended by friends and families of the players. Five pesos is the price for admission to the games, a worthwhile expense for an authentic Santa Rosalían experience (and premium photo-op) completely removed from any conventional tourist experience.

Our take: No doubt about it, Santa Rosalía is an unexpected tourist destination worthy of your time. This diamond in the rough will continue to grow on you with each hour you spend learning the ins and outs of its geography, culture, and people. The distinct European influence can be seen in the French colonial style of the town's wooden buildings, in the mining history that pervades the local society, and even in the light-skinned, blue-eyed features occasionally seen in some of the Santa Rosalían people. Its personality, rather than its looks, will win you over. Santa Rosalía is an interesting town full of an entirely unique breed of French Baja charm.

# ACKNOWLEDGEMENTS

We first and foremost want to acknowledge Alan Axelrod for fully dedicating himself and his resources to this project and allowing us to have this incredible opportunity. There would be no *Best Guide: Loreto* without him. For everything from the initial planning to the practicalities of living in Loreto to the editing, production, and publishing of the book, he was there directing us, supporting us, funding us, and rooting us on. Thank you, Alan (Dad) for never giving up on our vision for this book.

The biggest question we had when the idea for this book first arose was 'where will we stay?' Thanks to the generosity of Steve Ast (who was then manager of the Inn at Loreto Bay in Nopoló) and his faith in us to complete the project, we were able to reside in a beautiful hotel for the summer.

Once we got settled in Loreto, we needed a network of individuals who could answer our questions, show us around, give us accurate information we would have never gotten otherwise, and make our time in Loreto more efficient . . . and memorable. These people include:

Walter Cunningham was our most valuable resource in Loreto. As a local Loretano, he told us who to talk to, where to go, and what to do, and often times talked to those people, went to those places and did those things *with* us. This book wouldn't be the same without Walter (he's responsible for much sidebar material).

Other key people include Leah Wooten, the former concierge at the Inn at Loreto Bay, who shared with us all the practical information that made our research easier; Hector Jimenez, who was always around the hotel to answer our questions and allowed us to use his office equipment without hesitation; Raphael González, then head of construction for the Loreto Bay Company (and the friendliest Buckeye we know— Go Blue!), who helped us on numerous occasions to avoid all sorts of trouble; Cecilia Fischer and her amazing knowledge of the natural wonders of the area; Rob Cairns, who helped us systematically look at all land and sea activities and outfitters; and, of course, Veronica and the rest of the staff at the Inn at Loreto Bay, who we feel lucky to call our friends. ¡Gracias a ustedes!

Of course we cannot forget all of our friends in town: Bruce Williams at Dolphin Dive, Trudi Angell of Saddling South, Juve at Cormorant, Kathy at Adventure Baja, Jonotan—the best smoothie guy in all the land, and, finally, Chicho Valenzuela and Panchito Reyes at the gimnasio who trained Aaron and welcomed us into their boxing family. They are our best friends in Loreto, and we hope that's the way it remains.

On the technical end we want to thank Paulette Eickman, project manager and graphic designer extraordinaire who managed all the pieces of this project and made the book a reality; Doug Ogle for his terrific photography; Leslie Eliel, our amazing copy editor; Beth Chapple, our Spanish language editor and proofreader; Carolyn Acheson, our indexer, and Sara Axelrod and Nick Hughes, who contributed the write-ups on Santa Rosalía and Mulegé. We also want to especially thank Rikki and Jack Swenson who believed in our project and contributed their imagery to the book.

We have learned that it takes a lot more than a manuscript to make a book. Thanks to all of the people above and everyone else who made this book a reality.

*David Axelrod and Aaron Bodansky*

Author doing Loreto research.

Photo by Doug Ogle

# PHOTOGRAPHER CREDITS

### Trudi Angell, www.tourbaja.com

Trudi Angell has been exploring, operating tours and living on the Baja peninsula since 1976. Her company has set the standard for sea kayaking ecotours in the area of Loreto. Also, with 20 years traveling the peninsula by mule and trail she offers multi-day pack and hike trips to favorite rock art sites. More than tours, her adventures show you the culture and soul of the people of the sierra as you take a glimpse into the lifestyle of locals: traditional singing, music, and other trail rhythms. Trudi thanks family, friends and photographers for letting Paddling South, Pedaling South, and Saddling South use their inspiring photos. *(See pages 9, 115, 130, 131, 134, 136, 137, and 140.)*

### Dolphin Dive Center, www.dolphindivebaja.com

Bruce Williams and Susan Speck's images and articles have been published in magazines and calendars worldwide. Susan also authored the book *Diving Baja California*, by AquaQuest Publishing. They continue to lead dive expeditions throughout the world. Because of Loreto's surrounding islands, whale migrations, abundance of dolphins and unique marine life, the Sea of Cortés has become one of their favorite dive locations. For additional images and a complete guide to Baja California's best dive sites, look for Bruce and Susan's latest book entitled *Diving and Snorkeling the Sea of Cortez* available at Authorhouse.com. *(See pages 7 and 8.)*

### Tom Grey, www.pbase.com/tgrey

Tom Grey is an amateur bird photographer who lives in Stanford, California. Please visit www.pbase.com/tgrey to see more of Tom's bird images. *(See pages 141, 142, and 143.)*

### Jim Knowlton, www.jimknowlton.com

Jin Knowlton combines his passions for the ocean, photography and environmental protection to create work that he hopes will inspire people to appreciate and protect our ocean world. When not taking pictures of Humboldt squid, cameraman Jim Knowlton can be found playing near the ocean with his wife, Rocio, and their two boys, Diego and Santiago. View more of Jim's photos at www.jimknowlton.com. *(See page 6.)*

## Doug Ogle, www.dougoglephoto.com

Doug Ogle is a Seattle based professional photographer who has enjoyed working with a long list of corporate, nonprofit and creative clients. His passion for seeing, feeling and capturing the light at the right moment (Doug's words) is imperative for his location work and was especially valuable on assignment in Loreto. His love of Mexico and the warm people he has met there over the years has been the inspiration to create the images in this book. Doug was thrilled to join the brilliant team of Producers/Writers Alan and David Axelrod and Art Director/Designer Paulette Eickman in this gorgeous paradise for six days. *(See front and back covers and pages 10, 15, 16, 18, 24, 29, 30, 32, 35, 40, 42, 45, 47, 49, 52, 54, 57, 59, 66, 69, 70, 73, 74, 75, 78, 80, 83, 85, 86, 115, 126, 133, 144, 145, and 190.)*

## Jack & Rikki Swenson, www.BajaPhotos.com
## *Images That Fuel Conservation*

Jack and Rikki Swenson are professional wildlife and nature photographers who work as Photo Expedition Leaders for the Lindblad Expeditions/National Geographic alliance, guiding others to many of the world's wildest places. They created BajaPhotos.com to use their photography as a tool for conservation. BajaPhotos.com offers stunning images of the natural world from the Gulf of California and the Baja Peninsula. A percentage of all funds from licensing fees are donated annually to conservation organizations working in the region. Their work supports COBI (Communidad y Biodiversidad), Conservation International, GEA (Grupo Ecologista Antares), Grupo Tortuguero, Island Conservation, and Pro Peninsula. To view images, please visit BajaPhotos.com. *(See inside front cover and pages 3, 4, 5, 7, 124, 138, 139, and 142.)*

**Additional photos were taken by Alan Axelrod** *(pages 8, 22, 105, 176)*, **David Axelrod** *(page 168)*, **Sara Axelrod** *(55, 102, 150, 166, 170, 178)*, **Danzante Eco-Resort** *(page 165)*, **John Glascock** *(page 143)*, **and Matilde Sant'Ambrogio** *(page 187)*.

# INDEX

# INDEX

# INDEX

# INDEX

# INDEX

# INDEX

# INDEX

# BIBLIOGRAPHY

*Loreto Bay Guidebook* (Loreto Bay Company, 2007)

O'Neil, Ann and Don O'Neil, *Loreto, Baja California: First Mission and Capital of Spanish California* (Tío Press, Studio City, CA, 2001)

Peterson, Walt, *The Baja Adventure Book* (Wilderness Press, Berkeley, 2006)

Steinbeck, John, *The Log from The* Sea of Cortez (Penguin, 2000)

## ★ Mexico Highway 1 Mileage Table

| | Tijuana | Ensenada | San Quintín | El Rosario | Cataviña | Bahía de Los Angeles Jct. | Guerrero Negro | San Ignacio | Santa Rosalía | Mulegé | Loreto | Ciudad Constitución | La Paz | Cabo San Lucas |
|---|---|---|---|---|---|---|---|---|---|---|---|---|---|---|
| Ensenada | 70 / 112 | | | | | | | | | | | | | |
| San Quintín | 188 / 302 | 118 / 190 | | | | | | | | | | | | |
| El Rosario | 223 / 359 | 153 / 246 | 35 / 56 | | | | | | | | | | | |
| Cataviña | 299 / 482 | 229 / 369 | 112 / 179 | 76 / 123 | | | | | | | | | | |
| Bahía de Los Angeles Jct. | 364 / 585 | 294 / 473 | 176 / 283 | 141 / 226 | 64 / 103 | | | | | | | | | |
| Guerrero Negro | 448 / 720 | 378 / 608 | 260 / 418 | 225 / 362 | 148 / 239 | 84 / 135 | | | | | | | | |
| San Ignacio | 539 / 867 | 469 / 754 | 351 / 565 | 316 / 508 | 239 / 385 | 175 / 282 | 91 / 146 | | | | | | | |
| Santa Rosalía | 584 / 939 | 514 / 827 | 396 / 637 | 361 / 580 | 284 / 458 | 220 / 354 | 136 / 219 | 45 / 72 | | | | | | |
| Mulegé | 622 / 1001 | 552 / 888 | 434 / 699 | 399 / 642 | 323 / 519 | 258 / 416 | 174 / 280 | 83 / 134 | 38 / 62 | | | | | |
| Loreto | 708 / 1139 | 638 / 1026 | 520 / 837 | 485 / 780 | 408 / 657 | 344 / 554 | 260 / 419 | 169 / 272 | 124 / 200 | 86 / 138 | | | | |
| Ciudad Constitución | 795 / 1279 | 725 / 1167 | 607 / 977 | 572 / 921 | 496 / 798 | 432 / 694 | 347 / 559 | 257 / 413 | 212 / 340 | 173 / 279 | 88 / 141 | | | |
| La Paz | 925 / 1489 | 855 / 1376 | 737 / 1187 | 702 / 1130 | 626 / 1007 | 562 / 904 | 477 / 768 | 387 / 622 | 342 / 550 | 303 / 488 | 218 / 350 | 130 / 209 | | |
| Cabo San Lucas | 1061 / 1708 | 992 / 1596 | 874 / 1406 | 839 / 1350 | 762 / 1227 | 698 / 1123 | 614 / 988 | 523 / 842 | 478 / 769 | 440 / 707 | 354 / 570 | 266 / 429 | 136 / 220 | |

The upper black figures are miles and the lower orange figures are kilometers.